Praise for Robert M. Meisner and *Condo Living 2*:

"As the president of a large condominium association, I was greatly appreciative of Bob Meisner's initial exposé on condo life and management. His new edition expands the reader's insight and propels their knowledge to new heights. A must read for anyone thinking about serving on a condominium board or, for that matter, any type of community or homeowner association."

LATHUS HALL
PRESIDENT, GREENBROOKE PARKHOMES CONDOMINIUM ASSOCIATION

"Bob Meisner is the best at what he does, and his explanation of the needs and concerns of anyone thinking about buying a condominium or serving on the board of a condominium association is unmatched. Every developer should keep this by his bedside before venturing into the world of condominium development."

BERNIE GLIEBERMAN
DIRECTOR OF NEW BUSINESS OPPORTUNITIES, HOME RENEWAL SYSTEMS

"I wish we had known about this book before my wife and I purchased our condominium unit. Fortunately, we read it before selling our condo. The information clearly defines the selling and legal requirements, describes some major potential problems that can occur, and how to avoid them. It's a great resource filled with important tips."

CLARENCE MORGAN
FORMER PRESIDENT, CONDOMINIUM BOARD OF DIRECTORS

CONDO LIVING

2

THE AUTHORITATIVE GUIDE
to Buying, Selling, and
Operating a Condominium

BY ROBERT M. MEISNER, ESQ.

Illustrations by Marty Harris and Rob Graham

Momentum Books, L.L.C.
Royal Oak, Michigan

This book is dedicated to my two sons—Derek, the lawyer, and Randy, the doctor—and my grandchildren, Ellie, Zachary, Olivia, and Samantha.

Published by Momentum Books, L.L.C., a subsidiary of Hour Media, L.L.C.
117 West Third Street
Royal Oak, Michigan 48067
www.momentumbooks.com

Printed and bound in the U.S.A.

ISBN-13: 978-1-938018-01-5
LCCN: 2013931604

TABLE OF CONTENTS

1 | **PREFACE**
A Note to the Reader:
What's In a Name?
The Reality of Condo Living and Governance
It Takes All Kinds
About This Book

13 | **PART I: BUYING AND SELLING A CONDO**
15 | **CHAPTER 1: I'M BUYING *WHAT?***
Understanding Condos and Their Terms

27 | **CHAPTER 2: DO I KNOW MY RIGHTS?**
Understanding Local, State, and Federal Statutes and Regulations

35 | **CHAPTER 3: CONDO, SWEET CONDO**
Purchasing a Condo as Your Primary Residence
The Communal Living Model
Is a Condo Right for Me?
The First Step
It's Like Finding the Right Mate
You Mean I Will Own That, Too; or Gosh, I Don't Own That?
The Contract
Before You Sign

59 | **CHAPTER 4: LOCATION, LOCATION, LOCATION**
Purchasing a Condo As An Investment
Second Home vs. Investment Property
The Commercial Condominium
Mobile Home Condominiums
Campsite Condominiums
Mixed Use, Retail, and Hotel Condominiums
Hotels
Parking Lot Condominiums
Marina Condominiums

69 | **CHAPTER 5: THE BEST OF BOTH WORLDS**
Vacation Homes and Taxes

75 | **CHAPTER 6: CLOSING TIME**
Guidelines to Selling a Condo
Selling Guidelines
"As Is, Where Is," No Warranties
The Real Estate Closing
Tax Ramifications

91 | **CHAPTER 7: RENTERS BEWARE!**

Legal Issues for Co-owners—and Tenants

The Lease Agreement

The "Renters"

Bylaw Violations Begin

Legal Action is Taken

Self Help

Legal Nightmare

Lessons Learned

What a Tenant Should Know!

Stuck in the Middle

103 | **PART II: THE OPERATION OF A CONDOMINIUM ASSOCIATION**

105 | **CHAPTER 8: CAST OF CHARACTERS**

The Board of Directors

What Makes a Good Board?

Seeking Outside Help

Establishing Subcommittees

A Contrast

The Ideal Director

121 | **CHAPTER 9: THE MAN WITH THE PLAN**

The Developer and Transition to Co-owner Control

Preparing for the Turnover

Your Future is in Their Hands

The Learning Experience

Audits at the Turnover

The Financial Audit

The Legal Audit

The Physical Audit

The Operational Audit

137 | **CHAPTER 10: CHOOSING HIRED HELP**
The Condo Association Attorney, Managing Agent, CPA, and
Insurance Agent
 Picking the Right Attorney
 Selecting the Right Managing Agent or Type of Management
 Picking the Right CPA and Insurance Agent

155 | **CHAPTER 11: SKELETONS IN THE CLOSET**
Potential and Actual Problems for Condominium Associations

161 | **CHAPTER 12: CRIME AND PUNISHMENT**
Condo Rules Are Not Made to be Broken
 Rules and Restrictions
 Home Businesses / Right to Lease
 Activities
 Pets
 The Catch-All
 Children
 Cooking
 Motorcycles
 Retirement
 Know and Follow the Rules

171 | **CHAPTER 13: SHOW ME THE MONEY!**
Assessment Collection: The Lifeblood of the Association
 The College Student and the "Snowbirds"
 The Lien
 The Final Letter
 The Lawsuit
 The Judgment
 Judgment Collection
 Pay Your Dues

181 | **CHAPTER 14: EMPTY PROMISES**
When the Developer Walks Away from the Project

187 | **CHAPTER 15: FRISKY BUSINESS**
Condoms, Condominiums, and Conception
    The Noisy Neighbor
    The Hot Tub Party
    Children and Condos

195 | **CHAPTER 16: SEAL OF APPROVAL**
Why Most Condominium Projects Need FHA Certification
    Major Changes to FHA (1934 - 2009)
    Get FHA Certifies to Enhance Marketability!
    Updating Your Condominium Documents to Streamline the Process
    Recertify Every Two Years

205 | **PART III: SOUND ADVICE**
207 | **CHAPTER 17: WORDS OF WISDOM**
Final Thoughts on Condo Living
    A Proposed Solution
    Meisner's Maxims

227 | **CHAPTER 18: ASK THE GURUS**
Newspaper columns and anecdotes from legal beagles

247 | **EPILOGUE**
249 | **ACKNOWLEDGMENTS**
251 | **ABOUT THE AUTHOR**
253 | **INDEX**
261 | **REFERENCES**

PREFACE

The names and events depicted in this book are fictional and, although based on real-life experiences of the author, are not intended to describe any actual person, entity, or event. Any similarity to any person, living or dead, or to any entity or event, is purely coincidental. But if the shoe fits, wear it!

A NOTE TO THE READER:

Both men and women buy condos, but to ease the reader's burden, I will use "he" to stand for both except for occasional references to "he or she" in order to remind us that either gender could be involved.

WHAT'S IN A NAME?

Have you noticed that condominium developers often come up with the most idyllic names for condominium projects? Developers understandably try to paint the rosiest picture of condominium living, and one of the best marketing ideas is a name that conveys that attitude. Utopian sounding names, such as "Green Farms," "Pleasant Acres," "The Woods," "Windmill Pointe," "Oakwood Park," "Pebblecreek," "Greenbrooke," and "Streamwood" are common. Or the developer may invoke the names of places in old England, or other parts of Europe, to convey its marketing message. Names like "Coventry," "The Villas of Stonehenge," "Londonderry Downs," "English Colony," "Colonial Village," "Brittany," and "Le Chateau" convey an image of solitude, peacefulness, tranquility, and castle-like habitability.

We should stress truth in condominium labeling, as we already have truth in lending, truth in renting, and truth in packaging. Condominiums should be no different. In fact, I'd love to live in a condo that was honest enough to call itself "The Palaces of Bin Laden!"

Wouldn't it be more truthful if the condo developer, who is converting a run-down apartment complex into a condominium and selling the units "as is" and "without warranties," were to market his project as "The Leaning Tower," instead of "Fox and Hounds"? A condominium named "Lake in the Woods," known by the developer to have a history of erosion and pollution problems, probably would be more accurately named "Waste Disposal Gardens."

Perhaps developers ought to borrow names from great battles, such as "Waterloo," "The Bulge," or "The Alamo," to describe the confrontations that, no doubt, will occur among some residents of a condo. The Nazi-like attitude conveyed by some directors would lend itself to a project known as "Gestapo Gardens." And wouldn't it be more realistic if a condo populated with chronic malcontents, distraught with the actions of the directors no matter what they do, was referred to as "Nuthouse Villas" or "Freud Landings"?

Sure, it would hurt the developer's marketing program, but it might also convey a more realistic message to the prospective condominium purchaser. In fact, such changes would ultimately avoid litigation because purchasers would know exactly what they are getting into when they buy!

THE REALITY OF CONDO LIVING AND GOVERNANCE

Many readers will think I had perpetual heartburn and indigestion when I wrote my initial book and this updated and expanded exposé.

Again, my central theme is that condominium living is not for everyone. Condominium living is replete with pitfalls, trials, and tribulations. Anyone who is interested in buying a condominium, regardless of his socio-economic, religious, geographic, or age group, should be aware of the legal and practical aspects of life in a condominium.

What should be emphasized, as well, is that one must have a particular personality and disposition to enjoy condominium living. That conclusion would apply whether the prospective purchaser is single, retired, or married without children. (My focus on these groups is not intended to suggest condominiums should not be occupied, or cannot be enjoyed, by families with children. That is not, however, one of the most common types of condominium purchaser, since condominiums typically are either apartments or townhouses located in a confined setting that is not conducive to the rearing of large families, which typically require open spaces to play and run.)

"IT TAKES ALL KINDS"

Let's look for a moment at the three types of people most likely to consider buying a condo, and consider whether the condominium lifestyle is for them.

The first type of condo purchaser I will discuss is the single.

Mistakenly, and without the "advice of counsel," I bought a condominium during my divorce. Perhaps the trauma of the divorce temporarily asphyxiated my brain cells. Whatever the reason, I thought I could get along in a condominium project which had been managed for 15 years by residents who:

- Rarely sought legal advice (and when they did, called on residents of the condominium to give them "free" advice);

- Built up no reserve fund because a real estate agent thought it would increase the monthly assessment to the extent that the condominium would become unmarketable; and,

- Were more concerned about the landscaping program than repairing cracks in the walls of units.

Generally, however, single people find condominiums attractive because they will not have to worry about the exterior maintenance and will enjoy social and recreational amenities that may not be available to them in a single-family dwelling. Unlike a rental apartment, they expect their investment will build equity, which may be true in the right circumstances.

My experience as a single person living in a condominium is that these expectations may be realized if the other problems common to condominium living can be avoided. If you don't care how the association really works, so long as your grass is cut and the roof is fixed, then living in a condo may be the answer. Unfortunately, "carefree maintenance" is beneficial to a single person only if the association discharges its legal and fiduciary responsibilities for maintenance.

Moreover, the single person who decides to have wild parties in his condominium unit will soon find he is an unpopular resident and the target of letters or litigation, or both, brought by his neighbors or the condominium association. Finally, if the single person has a mind of his own and is concerned about the possibility of an abusive board of directors, he may smartly retreat to a single family detached home (not a site condominium) and stay out of the bureaucratic morass that frequently exists in condominium communities!

If the condominium project is composed primarily of retirees, the tolerance of the board of directors toward youthful singles may be a problem. I have experienced instances where singles have bought units in a retirement community only to be subjected to the consternation of neighbors, and eventually the board of directors, over the nighttime presence of male or female guests.

If you are a single person, are considering a condominium and have evaluated all of the other aspects of condominium living, make sure that you won't be a social outcast. In particular, make sure your lifestyle will mesh with the lifestyle of most other association members. In my experience, being single and living in a condo was not a problem from the standpoint of disturbances by my neighbors. However, I lived in a semi-detached townhouse separated from the adjoining townhouses by a common wall, a physical configuration that reduced the proximity of residents. By contrast, an apartment-style condominium, where people may live both above and below, may lead to noise problems ranging from dropped shoes to late-night parties.

At the risk of sounding chauvinistic, condominium living may be particularly good for a single woman who lacks the time, skills, or desire to maintain a single-family home on her own. The condominium may provide her with enhanced security and camaraderie, usually without the responsibility to cut the grass and perform exterior maintenance and repairs.

Retirees, the second group of condo purchasers, may find condominium living advantageous because they may, as they prefer, participate in, or dissociate themselves from, the affairs of the association community. Having been involved in such activities throughout their lives, they may now be looking for a time to rest. The risk, if these persons do not participate, is that they are deferring to persons whose life experiences and skills may not equip them to perform these responsibilities.

On the other hand, if the retiree is looking for a situation where the monthly assessments will not go up and there is no potential for controversy, condominium living may not be the answer. Eventually, the common elements will need to be repaired or replaced, and the monthly assessments may need to be increased, sometimes significantly, to meet these needs. The condominium that is composed primarily of retired people on fixed incomes may not be the place for a young married couple or a single person to invest, because the board, which presumably will be composed of retirees, may not be disposed to spend the money necessary to deal with the problems and long-term concerns of the condominium. In this book, I hope to make the reader aware of the practices of developers and condominium association boards which may lead to unexpected problems that produce conflict between the interests of these groups.

Things that seem simple and harmless on the surface may be a problem as well. For instance, if the retiree wants to plant flowers, he'd better make certain that the association doesn't have an absolute prohibition on the planting of flowers!

In general, condominiums that are dominated by persons of a single marital status, age group, or socio-economic group may be problematic, since the decisions of that association will tend to be parochial and reflective of the particular needs of that group.

For example, a condominium composed exclusively of retired corporate executives will not necessarily be well-managed or an enjoyable place to live. The "country club" mentality of the directors may not lend itself well to the operation of the association. Moreover, although the modern corporate executive may promote an atmosphere in which ideas are welcomed, corporate executives who encourage dissenting views remain rare.

A more diverse composition of members—some retirees, some newly married, some single, some affluent, and some of more limited means—creates a mix that is beneficial to the condominium's success. In short, a diversity of personalities is, in my experience, better for the success of the association.

An exception may be senior citizen housing, including condominium housing for retired persons. Here, like-minded residents may share their concerns and participate in the various social and recreational activities that are available, while excluding families with children, if they qualify under the amendment to the Federal Fair Housing Act of 1989. Even here, however, unique problems may arise because of the general unwillingness of senior citizens to spend the money necessary to properly operate the affairs of the association and repair and replace the common elements.

Condominium living is not for everyone. It is not for people who do not have the economic means to properly sustain the operation of the association and to deal with its problems. Perhaps apartment living for those people is more appropriate. Senior citizens who read this book should keep this in mind in making the decisions necessary to operate the affairs of the association.

We come at last to the third common type of condo purchaser: married couples without children. Having lived in an apartment, two condominiums, and several single-family suburban houses, I can unequivocally state that if you are going to raise a family, do so in a detached, single-family subdivision or site condominium rather than an apartment or attached condominium. This assumes, of course, that you have a choice. If you live in Manhattan, there is little chance of finding an affordable, single-family detached dwelling. If you live in Great Neck, Long Island, the circumstances may be different.

In the typical "traditional," or apartment-style, condominium, any exterior modifications, including basketball hoops and roof aerials, must be approved by the condominium board of directors. More significantly, kids make noise, want to play outside, have friends over, and engage in activities that other residents, particularly those who are senior citizens or who are childless, may find annoying and objectionable. (Keep in mind that most senior citizens have been through the child-rearing years and are no longer interested in dealing with its rigors, except for the occasional visit of their grandchildren on a Sunday afternoon.) Finally, a major problem in condominiums, from the standpoint of the board, is children who abuse the condominium premises.

It is no secret that many traditional condominium projects do not like children within their confines, and I frequently am requested to draft condominium document provisions barring them. Federal legislation barring discrimination on the basis of age has rendered such prohibitions unenforceable, with the exception of qualifying "senior citizen" communities (age 55 and older). Consequently, it is illegal for a developer or condominium association to preclude children from living in a condominium.

Nevertheless, there often develops a sub-current of discontent when someone with children buys an attached condominium unit. Unless you are buying a unit in a condominium with numerous young marrieds with children, you are best advised to examine very carefully whether living in a condominium with children is a viable option for you, notwithstanding federal laws that purportedly protect you.

This is not to say that people with families cannot bring them up in condominiums. Again, it depends on the pertinent state and federal laws, the physical structure of the condominium unit itself, the restrictions imposed on co-owners and the attitude of the board of directors and managing agent toward family activities.

If you have a choice of housing, raise your family instead in a single-family subdivision, where the restrictions are minimal and the open spaces greater. That is not to say that homeowner associations do not have clout concerning the enforcement of deed restrictions on single-family residents within that subdivision.

Still, the restrictions in a homeowner's subdivision are generally not as pervasive and encompassing as those found in a condominium, even if that condominium is a "site" condominium.

A "site" condominium is a form of condominium in which all, or a portion, of the land is subdivided and sold as individual building sites, or condominium units, on which a co-owner may construct a dwelling. To the casual observer, a site condominium unit may be indistinguishable from a subdivision lot. In the site condominium, both the interior and exterior of the dwelling, and the other improvements located on the building site, are maintained by the individual co-owner, and not the condominium association, although the condominium association usually will retain exterior aesthetic control.

In summary, condominium living can be beneficial and an enjoyable experience. A condominium unit can be financially rewarding and a good investment. Co-owners can avoid physical work, time and, in some instances, the expenses of maintaining a single-family, detached dwelling. Condominium living offers social, recreational, vocational, and psychological benefits to its inhabitants. It also can provide enhanced security, reduction of fixed costs, and additional amenities that would not normally be affordable to residents in other types of living environments. It can offer an opportunity to participate in a community governing structure while gaining self-fulfillment from the knowledge that one is making a contribution. It can offer residents a place to live that demands only a minimal commitment to the governing structure and to the maintenance of the condominium community. It can be all of these things, but only to the person who has the right temperament, personality and socio-economic standing for that condominium. The person who wishes the freedom to live in his dwelling and its environs as he sees fit, without interference from any quasi-municipal governing structure, is not such a person. A farm would be a better place for that person!

ABOUT THIS BOOK

It should already be apparent to the reader that, through my more than 40 years of experience as an attorney, I have established my own criteria for good condominium living. I have also lived in a number of condos and have been on a board of directors of a condo development. In the following pages of this updated text, I will share my opinions and guidelines as well as thoughts and the input of Bailley, the firm's legal beagle, and Joyleih, the firm's assistant legal beagle.

This book is organized as follows: Part One discusses the factors to be considered when selecting, buying, and selling a condominium. Part Two explains the management and operation of condominium associations, and Part Three contains word of wisdom. I have appended my updated maxims, which I have collected over the years in the hope of shedding some humorous light on my subject. I've also included representative columns from the *Observer & Eccentric* newspapers that I have authored for more than 35 years, and excerpts from the anecdotes of Bailley and Joyleih, our legal beagles.

Sincerely,

Bob Meisner, with Bailley and Joyleih joining in.

P.S. The cartoons were added in case you start to take me too seriously.

PART I   Buying and Selling a Condo

Condominium living is not for everyone. There are numerous factors to consider before taking the plunge. Here's how to select, buy, and sell a condo.

CHAPTER 1

I'm Buying *What?*
Understanding Condos and Their Terms

Since condominiums are the focus of this book, it would appear necessary to fully acquaint the reader with what a condominium really is, as opposed to what you may have seen in movies or on TV, read in a newspaper ad or on the Internet, or heard from a friend or relative who lives in one. You may even own a condominium but not have a realistic idea of the legal and practical aspects of condominium living.

Condominium is not a new concept in housing. The word "condominium" comes from a Latin word meaning "common ownership or control." The Romans had condominiums, and during the Middle Ages, they were popular in the walled cities of Western Europe. During the first half of the 20th century, several European countries enacted statutes or laws permitting condominiums.

Although a few condominiums existed in the United States as early as 1947, they were not authorized by any state statute prior to 1961. Now, most every state has enacted some form of statute regulating the formation and operation of condominiums. Initially, many states adopted, either totally or in substantial part, the Uniform Condominium Act, a model residential condominium act. In Michigan, for example, the Horizontal Real Property Act, enacted in 1963, was modeled upon the Uniform Condominium Act. Because this law proved inadequate to meet the needs of the fast-growing condominium industry, the Michigan Condominium Act was enacted in 1978 with later significant amendments in 1983, 2001, and 2002.

In many states, second-generation, and even third-generation, condominium statutes have been enacted to address problems that were not envisioned or properly dealt with in the original enabling legislation. Most condominium statutes are designed to regulate the rights and responsibilities between: 1) The purchaser of a condominium unit and the developer of the condominium project; and 2) The co-owner of a condominium unit and the association of co-owners.

The reader may ask, "How does a condominium differ from a cooperative?" A cooperative is a residential housing project that is owned by a cooperative association, usually a nonprofit corporation. When you buy an interest in a typical cooperative, you become the owner of shares of stock in the cooperative association that owns all of the real estate of the cooperative, including the residential units. Generally, you then enter into a proprietary lease with the cooperative association that allows you to occupy a residential unit. In short, you do not own the residential unit in which you live, but instead, you own a share of stock in the cooperative association and you rent your unit. While cooperatives have been popular in the Eastern cities and in Chicago, they have not caught on as a major form of residential development in other parts of the United States.

Before you purchase a condominium unit, it is important to understand what the purchaser of a condominium unit typically buys; namely, an undivided interest in common areas and a cubicle of space within a commonly owned project.

Ordinarily, condominium unit ownership means the exclusive individual ownership of the space inside the inner walls of an apartment, townhouse, or high-rise, and common ownership of the surrounding structures, hallways, and underlying land. This division between exclusive and common ownership exists regardless of the form or design of the condominium project.

Although the focus of this book is the residential condominium, the reader should keep in mind that there are many other types of condominiums. Commercial condominiums are extremely popular as office space for professionals, and high-rise or mid-rise buildings containing a combination of commercial and residential condominiums (lofts) now dot the major cities of our hemisphere. Industrial condominiums are utilized for warehousing and factory facilities. Mobile home condominiums are catching on throughout North America. And campsite condominiums are popular in recreational areas. Time-share condominiums are widely advertised in vacation spots around the world. There are even parking lot condominiums, not only in the center of major cities, but near football stadia and other sports facilities. Speaking of football stadia, Ford Field, the home of the Detroit Lions (never to win a Super Bowl, but the site of the 2006 Super Bowl), was developed as a condominium!

In the residential context, the "project," as it is often called, may take the physical form of a high-rise townhouse building containing two or more areas of exclusive individual ownership. The project may instead consist of two or more individually owned single-family, detached dwellings constructed on the commonly owned land. Or, in the site condominium context, the land and air space comprising the entire envelope of the building site, together with the physical structure, may be individually owned.

In a mobile home, campground, marina, cruise ship, or parking site condominium, the area of exclusive ownership may be limited to a cube of air space within which a mobile home, recreational vehicle, stateroom, or where a car is parked or a boat is anchored. The elements of common ownership might then be the utility systems and the land or water improvements, such as concrete pads in the mobile home park, piers in a marina, or a clubhouse in a recreational condominium.

The condominium unit, which is the portion of the condominium that the purchaser individually owns, is his or hers exclusively to decorate, maintain, live in, and use. Usually, everything else in the condominium project, that is, the exterior walls, the commonly owned land, the common hallways in an apartment style building, the recreational facilities, etc., constitute the "common elements," the commonly owned property of everyone who owns a condominium unit in the project. So, in effect, a "condominium" is nothing more than a form of ownership in which certain portions of the property are owned by ALL owners of the condominium project, namely, the "co-owners," as they are referred to in the condominium documents and most enabling statutes.

Some of these "common elements," such as patios, balconies, garages, and carport spaces, although owned by all co-owners, are limited and restricted in use to the co-owner of the condominium unit they serve and his family. These common elements are generally referred to as "limited common elements." Other "limited common elements," such as stairways or laundry facilities, may be limited and restricted to use by all residents who live in that building. The remainder of the common elements, such as the land itself, roads, green areas, recreational facilities, and, in some instances, the outer walls, foundations, roofs, and other structural elements of the building are typically designated as "general common elements." The general common elements are available for the use, at least theoretically, of everyone who has an ownership interest in the condominium project. Both the limited common elements and general common elements, however, remain the common property of all the co-owners in the project.

Before you purchase a condominium unit, you also should understand the roles of the various entities which, typically, are involved in its organization, ownership and operation, namely: 1) the developer; 2) the individual co-owner; 3) the association of co-owners; 4) the board of directors of the association of co-owners; and 5) the managing agent.

Too often, in my experience, the purchaser or resident of a condominium lacks an accurate understanding of his or her rights and/or responsibilities because he or she does not understand the respective roles, rights, and responsibilities of the persons involved in the development and operation of the condominium project.

The "developer" is the person who has organized the condominium project and is responsible under the state enabling statute for doing so. The description of the condominium, including the assignment of limited common elements and general common elements and the respective responsibilities for their maintenance, repair, and replacement, and the respective rights of the developer, co-owners, and association of co-owners, are contained in the condominium documents, which the developer is responsible to prepare.

The term "condominium documents" typically refers to:

* The "Declaration" (or "Master Deed," as it is referred to in Michigan and in the remainder of this book).

* The "Condominium Bylaws," which are part of the Master Deed and are the basic constitution of how the condominium project will operate and function.

- The "Subdivision Plan," another part of the Master Deed, which locates the condominium unit at a point in space, using surveyor's coordinates.

- The "Articles of Incorporation" or similar document necessary to establish the condominium association as a corporation under the applicable state corporation law.

- The "Corporate Bylaws," sometimes called "Association Bylaws," of the condominium association, which provide for the operation of the association, including details regarding officers, directors, meetings, order of business, and so forth. Sometimes, the Condominium Bylaws and the Association Bylaws are combined in a single document.

The "co-owner," as he or she is frequently referred to when purchasing a condominium unit, becomes a member of an "association of co-owners," or simply the "association" or "condominium association." The association may be any type of legal entity; generally, however, the association of co-owners is a non-profit corporation.

If the association is a corporation, it will have all the vestiges of any other corporation of that type organized in that particular state. Since most corporations have boards of directors or trustees, the association, no doubt, will have a board of directors elected by the members of the association to manage the affairs of the condominium project.

The board is vested with the power to manage its association's affairs. However, the board of directors must be distinguished from the officers of the association, as this is one of the most frequently confused aspects of condominium operation. Frequently, the officers and directors are the same individuals, but the directors, unlike the officers, are elected by the members of the association and have the authority to run the association through a vote of the board. The officers merely operate and serve at the whim of the board of directors, are generally appointed by the board of directors, can be removed by a vote of the board of directors, and only have the power given to them by the Bylaws and Board Resolution.

When one takes title to his or her condominium unit, he or she, as a co-owner, becomes a voting member of the association. The weight given the vote of each co-owner as a member of the association is normally determined by the "percentage of value" assigned to his condominium unit in the Master Deed.

The Master Deed and/or Bylaws will provide for what party is responsible for monitoring certain aspects of the condo project. Generally, the association will be responsible to govern and maintain the common elements in the condominium project. However, the responsibility to maintain, repair and/or replace the common elements, particularly those which are limited common elements, may not be placed exclusively on the association of co-owners but, rather, in some instances, is imposed upon the individual co-owner(s) themselves.

For instance, while the association generally is responsible to maintain, repair and replace the general common elements, each co-owner typically is responsible for the maintenance and upkeep of the interior of his own unit and, perhaps, certain limited common elements assigned to his unit. (In a "site" condominium, the co-owner owns, and generally will be responsible to maintain, repair and replace both his dwelling and the exterior areas of the unit.)

Obviously, your condominium documents must be read carefully to understand which parts of your condominium are designated as units, limited common elements, or general common elements, and the extent to which the association is responsible for their maintenance, repair and/or replacement.

The association's management skill and diligence (or lack thereof) may have a significant impact upon its members. Keep in mind that the association is usually responsible for the maintenance of all portions of the condominium, other than the condominium units, such as the hallways, lobbies, building exteriors, landscaping, snow removal, trash pickup, and street maintenance (if the roads are private), and for the general operation of the common elements, including the recreational facilities, heating plant, water or electric systems, and the like. These tasks often are performed through a management firm, administrator or manager hired by the association board or, in some instances, by the co-owners themselves, if the condominium is "self-managed."

The "management company" or "managing agent," should the nonprofit corporation wish to hire one, is the entity that assists the board of directors in carrying out its responsibilities in managing the affairs of the condominium association. The managing agent may (and, while the developer is in control of the association at the initial stages of the project, typically will) be the developer or an affiliate of the developer.

Beware of situations where the developer is managing the condominium project either directly or through a subsidiary corporation. That frequently results in substantial abuse, which many condominium statutes allow to happen without adequate protections. In Michigan, the condominium association, after the nondeveloper co-owners obtain the right to elect a majority of the directors, generally can terminate any contracts with the developer that were made while the developer was in control of the association. This includes any long-term management contracts that were entered into with the developer or an affiliate of the developer.

Returning to the association, each co-owner pays a periodic fee, usually monthly, generally referred to as an "assessment," to defray the cost of services rendered by the association. On a yearly basis, the board of directors of the association will determine how much money it will need to run the affairs of the condominium in a budget. It then will divide the cost of operation among association members based upon the formula required by the condominium documents. The weight of the co-owner's vote and his financial obligation to support the association may not be the same; typically, however, the percentage of value (i.e. the ownership interest of the co-owner in the common elements) also is used to determine the percentage of the total assessment, as determined by the budget, that one will have to pay to the association on an annual basis.

Special assessments may be made by the board of directors to cover unexpected operational expenditures and repairs; but generally, any substantial increase by way of a special assessment for capital improvements or the like must be approved by a specified vote of the co-owners. Condominium bylaws typically set a dollar or subject matter limit on additional assessments that may be approved by the board of directors without a vote of the co-owners.

Provisions imposing late charges and other penalties for not paying assessments are commonly found in the condominium documents. Additionally, if one mortgages a unit, he may be required to notify the association of the name of the lender who is holding the mortgage and, after default in the payment of assessments, the association may have to inform the mortgage holder of any unpaid assessments due for the unit.

What many purchasers do not realize is that many condominium statutes grant to the association a lien against the condominium unit for unpaid assessments. This lien may be foreclosed in the same way a mortgage holder does after a default in the payment of mortgage payments. A foreclosure could result in the forced sale of the unit at public sale or auction and a loss of the unit to the association or other successful bidder.

The association has a great deal of power, not only to enforce the documents as they relate to the collection of assessments, but also to determine how you can live and what freedoms you have to enjoy your condominium unit and the project.

For instance, there may be restrictions on the use of a unit that can be enforced by the association. These may include such things as restrictions on pets, the selling or renting of a unit, the planting of flowers, posting of signs, and the parking of cars. The association may also have the right to set rules for the use of the recreational facilities and other common elements. It usually has the right to require approval of proposed modifications one may wish to make to the exterior or structural components of his unit. The subject of restrictions will be discussed in another chapter of this book.

I will also discuss in a subsequent chapter why it is important that you determine "who's in charge" of the association. As previously noted, the association is governed by a board of directors. The developer and/or its designees have the right to appoint the initial members of the board of directors who will run the association until the time prescribed by statute and/or the condominium documents as the date on which control of the nonprofit corporation must be turned over to the non-developer co-owners. This "transition of control" typically takes place after a sufficient percentage of units in the project have been sold or a certain amount of time has elapsed. During this period, the developer, through his appointees to the board of directors, determines the amount of assessments that will have to be paid by the co-owners in the project. The developer also may be able to amend the condominium documents without the approval of the co-owners, so long as the amendment does not "materially" affect the rights of the co-owners, again dependent upon the respective state enabling statute.

In many respects, a condominium operates as a stand-alone community. In fact, the co-owners also must adhere to the zoning and other ordinances of the city or township of which the condominium is a part. Moreover, the condominium may be a part of a larger development, such as a Planned Unit Development (PUD). A PUD is a scheme of development which may include different forms of development—such as some, or all, of a cooperative, a condominium, a traditional subdivision, a recreational facility, a commercial office project, and retail space—within a geographic area. A "community association," as that term is generally used, is an organization established to manage and maintain such a multi-use community. For example, a community association may be formed to manage, provide common services to and maintain architectural control over the PUD, which includes a residential condominium, a retail "strip" mall and commercial office space. Similarly, an "umbrella" community association may provide services, such as administration and maintenance, to a group of subdivisions or condominiums or both that share the use of roads, utilities, or recreational amenities.

It is not my purpose in this book to provide a legal analysis of all the types of entities with which you may become involved when buying a condominium. But you should be familiar with all of the types of entities with which you are likely to become legally involved when you buy a condominium unit, ranging from the "umbrella community association" to the developer and management company.

It is the interrelationship between the condominium association, its board of directors, its management agent, if any, and the co-owners that will be the focal point of much of the discussion in the chapters that follow. They will show how you, as a prospective purchaser, present co-owner, or board member, can learn to deal with the complexities of these interrelationships.

CHAPTER **2** | # Do I Know My Rights?
Understanding Local, State, and
Federal Statutes and Regulation

As a prospective condominium purchaser or a director of a condominium association, one should at least have a general knowledge of the applicable local, state, and federal statutes and regulations applicable to the condominium in question.

In many states, first-generation condominium statutes created a regulatory body or agency to administer the sale and development of condominiums. The rationale for involving a state regulatory body is that the sale of a condominium is analogous to a security and that some form of state regulation of its sale is necessary in order to protect the purchaser. In Michigan, for example, the Horizontal Real Property Act of 1963 established powers in an administrator who was an employee of the Michigan Department of Commerce and was assigned the responsibility to review all development and sales documents incidental to the sale of interests in a condominium project by a developer. The developer was required to obtain a permit to sell condominium units before sales transactions could be consummated in the state. The condominium master deed, condominium and association bylaws, and sales and advertising materials were required to be approved by the Department of Commerce, Condominium Section, before they could be used by a developer. State administrative regulation of condominiums was intended to ensure that condominium developers adhered to the dictates of the statute, that unreasonable or unconscionable restrictions or provisions were not placed in the condominium documents by unscrupulous developers and their lawyers, and that there was some uniformity in condominium document content.

In general, state regulation of the sale of condominiums worked well. It served as a filtering process to eliminate many bad developers and bad condominium documents. In Michigan, the state regulatory body had a great deal of power to ensure that the developer met commitments made when it sold condominium units—including adequate funding of the condominium association, the completion of promised amenities, and the correction of defects and deficiencies in the condominium project.

Those who opposed state regulation of condominiums complained that the regulatory process was unnecessarily time-consuming and expensive for the developer. Others complained that influential developers and/or their lawyers received favored, preferential treatment from state regulators. Still others complained that state regulatory agency approval gave the purchaser a false sense of security concerning the quality and fairness of condominium documents that had received agency approval. Through a step-by-step process, the Michigan state regulatory body was relieved of most of its pre-sale responsibilities for condominiums. By 1983, the result was "deregulation" of the sale of condominiums. Most other states also have embraced deregulation. Interestingly enough, Florida, by way of the Division of Florida Condominiums, Timeshares, and Mobile Homes, and California, by way of the California Department of Real Estate, which are perhaps the two states with the most condominiums, continue to heavily regulate the sale and development of condominiums. Whether condominium deregulation is a good idea is subject to political, as well as legal, debate. Both sides have strong arguments.

The statutes of "deregulated" states give the purchaser or association very little, if any, administrative recourse against the inexperienced or unscrupulous developer who fails to comply with the basic requirements of the condominium statute and/or basic tenets of fundamental fairness. Redress is left to the courts, which is likely to be both expensive and time-consuming.

The suggestion that a purchaser or association may obtain redress by pursuing an action seeking revocation of the developer's builder or real estate broker license is often wishful thinking. Rarely is a developer's builder or real estate broker license revoked, and then only after long, drawn-out proceedings that provide the association or disgruntled purchaser a less immediate and effective remedy than is even available through the court system.

On the other hand, condominium deregulation has encouraged the enhanced development of property, since it can be accomplished more quickly and less expensively than before deregulation. Moreover, the "built-in" protections against developer abuse that are found in most second-generation condominium statutes have proven more effective in curbing developer abuse than many, including me, initially believed.

Developers who meet their responsibilities can succeed without undue governmental interference under condominium deregulation. However, it is important that such developers play a leadership role in policing their industry. If the excesses of "bad" developers are not voluntarily curbed through industry pressure, an avalanche of anger and protest may erupt when the abuses come to light, with the result that legislatures may "roll back" deregulation to ensure that essential consumer rights are protected. The pendulum may swing back to the regulation of condominiums if developers abuse their prerogatives or if "good" developers fail to police the excesses of "bad" developers.

There are, I fear, thousands of instances in which condominium documents recorded in "deregulated" states are not in conformity with the statute or are of blatantly poor quality. I have seen situations where condominium projects have been expanded or contracted beyond the permissible statutory period, or where the subdivision plan drawings required by statute were never prepared or recorded, and, yet, mortgage and title companies lent money and issued title policies for the sale of units. I have seen overbearing and even unscrupulous clauses added to condominium documents without objection or outcry by the purchaser or the condominium association.

From the perspective of the prospective purchaser or association director, what is important is that they do their "homework" and know exactly what are their state and local regulatory rights and remedies. The state condominium law may afford remedies, notwithstanding that the state has gone to deregulation. There may be another statute or a municipal ordinance in effect that the developer did not follow. There may be, for example, money which was posted by the developer as a bond to ensure completion, and which is now available to the association or purchasers of a condominium.

The local municipality may assist the association by holding back additional building permits until the developer complies with site or code requirements for the units already constructed, or there may be a municipal ban on smoking in the condominium as is the case in San Rafael, California.

Finally, consumer protection laws of more general application may establish the potential for significant civil and, in some instances, criminal penalties.

As a practical matter, you first should determine whether the state or municipality in which you are buying a condominium, or in which the association you serve is located, retains regulatory power over the sale and development of condominiums and the subsequent operation of their associations. Keep in mind that there are states with loosely defined condominium statutes which lack specific parameters regulating the development of condos.

In general, the more statutory law there is in your state, and the more case law concerning the sale and operation of condominiums, the more accurate that the experienced community association practitioner will be in ascertaining the probability of your success against the "bad" developer. The community association practitioner in Florida probably has a better grasp of the law, and consequently the probable result, than does the practitioner in a state where there is no comprehensive condominium statute, no body of case law, and/or no strong state regulatory body.

A person residing in a condo and, especially, members of the board of directors and others administering the condo project or assisting the board of directors should also become familiar with certain applicable federal laws, including, without limitation, the Federal Fair Housing Amendments protecting against discrimination in housing, the Service members Civil Relief Act protecting persons in the military, and the Federal Communications Commission Rules promulgated under the Federal Telecommunications Act of 1996 which protect citizens' rights to receive telecommunication reception in their condominium setting, with certain limited restrictions.

What also should not be underestimated is that the condominium association, sometimes comprised of hundreds of individuals, has political and economic power. That power should be exerted when dealing with national, state, and local agencies. In addition, when condominium associations band together to promote their views on such matters as taxation and community services, they may wield substantial power because of the sheer numbers available to them.

Too often, associations are instead dysfunctional in coordinating their efforts, not only among themselves, but in joining groups to influence particular problems. Fortunately, there are exceptions at both the national and state level.

At the national level, the Community Associations Institute, founded in 1975 and headquartered in Alexandria, Virginia, serves as a catalyst to provide education for all participants in the condominium industry, including developers, managers, public interest officials, condominium professionals, and community association organizations.

In Michigan, the United Condominium Owners of Michigan was formed in 1973 to advance the interests of condominiums in the state. While not a lobby group per se, it is a voluntary nonprofit organization formed to educate condominium associations and their directors in advancing the interests of condominiums regarding proposals for legislation and general enhancement of condominium living.

The condominium association, developer, or purchaser should inquire about and support such local, state, and national organizations. Developers have tended to gravitate toward organizations such as the local builder's or apartment owner's association to advance their interests. There is a need for organizations to represent all interests involved in the condominium industry. If these organizations are supported and flourish, a better condominium product will result for all concerned!

In suggesting that there are remedies available at the state, local, and national levels, I emphasize that there are no shortcut answers to resolving the problems of condominium development and living. For example, regarding construction problems, associations and co-owners often have sought a quick-fix remedy in order to avoid the cost and delay of the judicial process and, for that matter, the administrative process. They accept the promises of the developer even though they know all too well, based on the developer's track record, that such promises are not likely to be fulfilled. They may write their congressperson, their state legislator, their mayor or the local building inspector to obtain redress. (Sometimes, redress may be obtained through the intervention of the local building official, so I do not mean to discourage exploration of this avenue.)

The aggrieved person usually finds that he is "spinning his wheels" when he seeks redress from a politician who does not have direct jurisdiction or control. Writing your U.S. Senator about a roof leak in your condo will more than likely not result in any meaningful resolution of the problem. Although the senator may be kind enough to respond to your letter and direct you to a local consumer protection agency, generally that will not result in an adequate or expeditious resolution of your problem.

It may be that available remedies should be exercised in combination to redress the problem. For example, it may be appropriate to threaten legal proceedings and, at the same time, request state administrative intervention. Similarly, if the local building inspector is sympathetic to the association's plight, he may exert pressure upon the developer to resolve the problems. Occasionally, the municipality may intervene in the condominium project to protect the interests of the municipality, which, in turn, may be beneficial to the interest of the purchaser or association. Common sense should enter into the picture when identifying the best remedy available to the association or aggrieved person with the help of an experienced community association attorney.

CHAPTER 3

Condo, Sweet Condo
Purchasing a Condo as Your
Primary Residence

THE COMMUNAL LIVING MODEL

One who considers condominium living soon recognizes that he must become a student of communal living. Communal living in our society exists in a number of forms. Shared responsibility for the operation of a particular geographic environment is not a unique concept, and the problems of inter-relationships between individuals confined within a geographic boundary also are not unique. Typical examples of communal living range from depersonalized arrangements, such as jails, hospitals, health clubs, and country clubs, to personalized living arrangements, such as community associations, PUDs, apartments, residence halls, neighborhood associations, trailer parks, co-housing communities, and marina boat parks.

If one wishes to understand the real notion of a condominium, one must be an observer of other types of communal living. To a varying degree, basic precepts of human interplay within an institutional environment, such as a jail, hospital, or health club, apply as well to condominium living insofar as there needs to be limitations on the liberties of persons living in proximity and sharing common facilities.

I have often believed that an exhaustive psychological background in the phenomena of group behavior, particularly as it relates to communal living models, would assist anyone in dealing with condominiums. People change when they operate in a communal environment. For instance, the collective decision of the board of directors of a condominium association often will not reflect the individual feelings of its members, who, if separately polled on an issue, might reach a different result. (People would likely become more honest about their true feelings or they might become more dictatorial.) Many use the condominium mode of living as an opportunity to lie back and relax, or to release their pent-up aggressions or frustrations. This phenomenon has been confirmed in research discussions with community association practitioners across the 50 states. It's clear to me that additional research is needed to explore the phenomenon of condominium living and governance in an effort to attempt to isolate and interpret the behavioral characteristics that permeate condominium operations.

The problems of senior housing and assisted living facilities also apply to condominiums, particularly when people are not able to take care of themselves. This becomes an increasing problem as our population ages. The board of directors of a condominium association must struggle with the needs of people who are disabled, physically or mentally infirm, or are otherwise unable or unwilling to live with their neighbors in an unattended, congenial, and/or law-abiding manner.

Similarly, the college dormitory is a place of active social interaction. The study of dormitory living alone can benefit the researcher analyzing condominium operation. That some condominium projects include numbers of college students who live there as owners or tenants poses other unique problems to the condominium's operation.

The extent to which low-income housing attributes and characteristics apply to the condominium model depends on the social-economic groups living in the condominium. In a low-income situation, even a modest increase in the assessments can pose serious problems to the co-owners and threaten the successful operation of the condominium association. Too frequently, a person of minimal means purchases a condominium, through subsidy or otherwise, with a minimal or no down payment and without an appreciation of the true costs required to operate and maintain the condominium; witness the mortgage meltdown of the late 2000s.

A fundamental question is whether the condominium is suitable as a form of low-income housing. While condominium boards may try to adjust to an increase in their operating costs by spreading needed additional or special assessments over an extended period, or do nothing and let the project deteriorate, some co-owners will still not be able to keep up and will either sell or default to the mortgage company and/or the condominium association. In any event, it is clear that the condominium association must remain economically self-sustaining, cannot function as a welfare agency, and cannot operate at the level of the lowest common denominator.

I have attempted in this section to introduce issues and point to life situations which are, at least in certain respects, comparable to life in a condominium. However, the answer to the group behavior dynamics of a condominium remains ripe for discussion. Send me your comments at www.meisner-law.com.

IS A CONDO RIGHT FOR ME?

First, a word about the acceptability of condominiums in your locale. Condominiums are not popular everywhere. For example, co-ops are considered to be housing for the elite and affluent in New York, while in other municipalities, co-ops are synonymous with subsidized "low income" housing. Generally, however, condominiums have now been accepted by both the public and the lending institutions that fund their purchase.

Newspaper and Internet ads, TV and radio spots, glossy brochures, and even your best friends may extol the virtues of living in a condominium, either as a primary or secondary residence. Advertising jingles and hype create the illusion of the condominium as "carefree living." To the contrary, I have discerned over my years of experiences, both as a counselor to and as a resident of condominiums, that condominium living is more accurately described as "careful living."

If the prospective purchaser of a condominium learns anything from this book, it should be the importance of adequate preparation and analysis before one buys a condominium. Once the purchase has been made, the purchaser is legally committed to the condominium "concept," and his choices are limited to the resale or leasing of his unit, or to a change in his personality, philosophy, and way of life that will conform to the condominium "concept."

What type of person is suited to condominium living? Perhaps the easiest way to answer the question is to describe the person who is *not* suited to condominium living.

As previously noted, attached condominium living generally is not suited to large families with young children who will wish to play with dogs that will need to be walked or multiple automobiles that will need to be parked or stored.

Condominium living is not for the person who:

• Is used to a farm environment;

- Wants a sprawling, single-family lot; or

- Desires to plant trees, decorate the exterior of his home, put up a large outside satellite dish on a general common element, or enlarge the size of his patio or deck without the permission of "big brother."

Condominium living is not for the person who is unwilling to follow restrictions on the type of vehicle he may drive, the number of animals he may nurture, the parties he may have, the additional persons who may reside at the condominium, and the like. Condominium living also is not for the person who is unwilling to spend large sums of money to maintain the exterior of his home because he does not care how it looks. In short, condominium living is not for the avid supporter of the American Civil Liberties Union! If you wish to live in a condominium, you must be prepared to give up a portion of the liberties, and the flexibility of lifestyle, which you might enjoy in a single-family, detached dwelling. If you are not such a person, you may wish to reconsider the condominium as a form of ownership and mode of living.

Conversely, condominium living may be the perfect answer for the person who wants to increase the amount of property and amenities he can afford by reducing his price per square foot; who wishes to delegate to others the obligations of maintenance, repair, and replacement of exterior and common areas; who is willing to abide by and embraces restrictions, rules, and regulations; and who wishes to enhance his social or recreational opportunities at a minimum cost.

In order to determine whether you are a good candidate for condominium living, you must understand what it is all about. That, of course, requires that you have read this revised book at least four times. For only then will you fully recognize the benefits—and the detriments—of condominium living!

I have assumed that you are planning to reside in your

condominium. Condominiums for investment, as well as recreational condominiums, will be discussed in later chapters. If you buy a condominium unit and plan on living in it as your primary residence, you obviously want to be reasonably sure that you are going to enjoy living there. Don't forget the basics, including whether you can stand to live with someone living directly above or next to you.

While you may have the option to rent out the condominium unit, depending upon the condominium restrictions, you should assume when you buy that you will be living there for an indefinite period. Given those considerations, it is essential that you understand the dynamics of condominium living, generally, and of the specific condominium project you are considering.

Those of us who are involved in the condominium industry will always agree on at least one thing. The biggest problem is that condominium purchasers do not know what it's really like to live in a condominium and do not have a clear understanding of what their responsibilities and obligations are as a member of the association. For some reason, most condominium owners choose to not read the documents, choose to not secure the assistance of qualified professional advisers who understand and can interpret the documents, or, if they have done so, conveniently forget what they have been told and do not wish to follow.

If, on the other hand, the prospective purchaser does what he is supposed to do to acquaint himself with the facts of condominium living and, in particular, the material facts about the project, not only will he be a more enlightened purchaser and a better condominium resident, but the condominium as a whole will be enhanced by his very presence. There would be one less person who has purchased a condo who has no business living in one!

THE FIRST STEP

What should a person interested in the purchase of a condominium do first? As with any purchase, the purchaser should consider the reasons he or she is considering a condominium and the price he or she can afford to pay. For example, a single person may consider moving to a condominium from an apartment because he or she believes that the time constraints, occasioned by his or her career or school, prevent him or her from caring for a home. Therefore, desiring to build up equity as opposed to paying rent may cause him or her to find the purchase of a condominium an attractive alternative. It may also give him or her an opportunity to meet other people through the condominium association, which may provide social, recreational, business, or even political contacts in the community.

The retiree may look at a condominium as a place he can live in relative comfort, free of the obligation to care for the yard, plow the snow, or worry about roof repairs. The condominium also may benefit the childless couple that does not have the money to buy a sprawling residence, but wishes to take advantage of the amenities provided by the condominium project, which may include a clubhouse, pool, exercise room, or jogging path.

Condominiums come in all locations, sizes, and varieties. Location, as with any piece of real estate, is one key to a successful condominium purchase. A particular condominium may be ideal for one couple or single, but not for another couple or single. For example, a high-rise condominium in downtown Chicago may offer the benefits of an urban center to a single person or an appropriate couple, while a townhouse condominium in the affluent Michigan suburb of Bloomfield Hills might be more appropriate to the person who prefers a suburban setting.

Price also will be a factor. Before choosing a particular condominium, the purchaser should consider similar condominiums that are available and compare the cost of single-family homes in the vicinity in which he or she wishes to locate. An additional consideration may be whether to buy "new" from the developer or to purchase a "used" unit in an established or "conversion" condominium project.

The time when you buy into the condominium project, particularly if you are buying from the developer, may have a bearing
on the purchase price as well as your decision to buy the unit. For
example, if you are living in the apartment building that is about
to be converted, you may have rights under state law to preserve
your apartment status for a period of time. In some instances,
depending on your age and whether or not you are a person with
a disability, this may be a period of years. If so, you may be
offered discounts by the developer to buy the condominium unit
in which you live. In the case of new construction, you may be
offered a pre-construction price that, presumably, will be less
than the price at which units will be offered to later purchasers.
You also may be offered additional amenities at a reduced price,
or without additional charge, or may be given a break on mortgage financing.

Whether you should pay for your unit with cash or borrowed
funds depends on economic considerations that are beyond the
scope of this book, other than to suggest that you should consult
with your financial planner or investment counselor as to whether
it would be more beneficial for you to invest all cash in the condominium or to partially finance it. You should consider factors
of inflation, the availability of cash reserves to you, the alternate
potential investments that are available to you with the cash that
you would use to purchase the condominium, the cost of bor-
rowing money, and the credit and psychological ramifications to
you of debt, if relevant.

A word about new construction versus a "conversion" condominium is appropriate here. A conversion condo is a project in
which the units have been occupied in some form, other than a
condominium, before the conversion by the developer. An example would be an apartment building that has been converted into
a condominium. The apartment units, obviously, are not new, and
are generally sold on an "as is" basis. Beware!

The law in most states, as in Michigan, imposes different

responsibilities on the developers of "new construction" versus "conversion" condominiums. Over the years, there has been considerable abuse in situations where condominium converters made only cosmetic changes to the existing buildings and sold the units and common areas "as is," suggesting to their naive purchasers either that there were no serious problems in the condominium project or that they did not know the real condition of the buildings and amenities.

Too often, what has happened is that the purchasers of units later discovered serious problems in the condominium project (particularly the common elements, which the purchaser seldom examines) and found that the association coffers contained inadequate funds to fix them. When the developer hides behind the "as is" disclaimer in its purchase agreement or disclosure statement, the condominium association is faced with raising funds through additional or special assessments before it can repair or replace substantially deteriorated condominium common areas and/or to seek legal redress.

Some municipalities have local ordinances that require the developer to provide an inspection report to the purchaser of a conversion project. Your lawyer should know whether there are any statutes that require the developer to provide you with an inspection report concerning the premises.

You should recognize that even if an inspection of the roofs, exterior, and structural elements were available, it may not reveal current defects since they are not "new" and their remaining useful life may be in question. For instance, roofs that may have been on for 15 years may fail within a few years, and there may be insufficient funds set aside in reserve to replace them.

In the case of a conversion condominium, it is vital that the purchaser understand that, although local building authorities may have inspected the building's heating, plumbing, and electrical systems, together with its roofing and structural supports, the inspection generally will not include a determination of the condition of other elements of the project. Additionally, it is important to remember that a local building authority inspection (if any is required) of a conversion condominium may only apply the construction codes that were in effect at the time the structure was originally erected or remodeled. If so, building authority approval of the building may provide no assurance that the building conforms to the current construction codes. (Any extensive remodeling done at the time of conversion, however, generally must meet current construction standards.)

The developer generally does not assume responsibility for the project when it is offered "as is." Consequently, you need to personally inspect not only the condominium unit you wish to purchase, but be cognizant of the condition of the buildings and other common elements of the condominium in order to determine their adequacy and condition.

In the conversion condo, the developer should be expected to provide you with a "Disclaimer of Warranties," wherein it attempts to reaffirm that the condominium project is being sold "as is, where is"; that there are no warranties, express or implied, of any kind made with regard to pre-existing building elements; and that the purchaser may be required to contribute substantial sums of money for condominium association assessments for the repair and replacement of common elements at some future time.

Unfortunately, most prospective purchasers never really understand or comprehend this language, or perhaps they never even read it. This is exacerbated by the fact that the selling broker may be telling the condominium purchaser how cheap it will be to live in the condominium project; how the developer is honorable and has had years of experience in converting condos; how beautiful the grass has been manicured and the how nice the streets look (has the developer put an asphalt blacktop coat over a concrete road with material subsurface defects?); and that the advertised assessment should be more than adequate to fund the reserves and meet annual expenses, particularly since the developer has already contributed $5,000 for that purpose! In Michigan, a developer of a conversion condominium is obligated to disclose the physical condition of the condominium if he knows it. Many developers claim in the disclosure statement that they do not know. If you see that statement, BEWARE!

New construction, of course, has its own problems. With any new construction, one normally should expect that there will be certain problems. While the law generally recognizes implied warranties regarding habitability and fitness of the condominium units and common elements, developers generally will limit their economic exposure by placing limits on the extent, scope, and duration of the warranty they provide to purchasers. Typically, a one-year limited warranty is given to a purchaser, which is really not an awful lot of time to determine the scope and magnitude of the problems that may be latent in the construction of the project.

One minor advantage to a conversion condominium may be that the buildings have been purportedly inspected by the developer (or by an engineer hired by the developer to survey the major component parts of the project, assuming that he has truthfully and fully disclosed the condition of same) and many of the initial construction "bugs" have been discovered and, presumably, corrected. In new construction, the developer may have done an admirable job in building the units. However, the condominium may not be totally complete when you consider buying. You may be faced with construction traffic and debris for three or four years, if then, while the remainder of the condominium project is completed and all bugs are corrected.

In a conversion condominium, the units generally will have been refurbished and will be available for occupancy immediately. In a new construction condominium, the developer may construct units in phases, for various reasons, including economic and legal, and you may be subjected to delays before your particular unit is completed.

After careful deliberation, you may decide that you would prefer to buy a "resale" condominium, rather than purchase a unit from the developer of a "new construction" or "conversion" project. Even if this is the case, you should investigate the history of the condominium project, that is, was it "new construction" or a "conversion" when it was established? Simply put, the more you know about the history of the development, the happier you will be, assuming you have made a reasonable business decision to buy a condominium in the first place and the condominium that you buy is the one for you!

If you buy a condominium from a developer, you generally will benefit from the protections afforded by state statute and/or the common law to the initial purchasers of condominium units, even in a state that has "deregulated" the development and sale of new condominiums. Conversely, for a resale condominium, there probably will be no state statutory law specific to the sale of condominiums, although general statutes or bodies of case law that would apply to the resale of any residential real estate will apply.

Occasionally, brokers will insert a provision in a purchase agreement for a "resale" condominium that obligates the purchaser to reimburse the seller for his so-called "owner's equity" in the condominium and/or condominium association. Presumably, the provision contemplates that the condominium owners have built up some equity over the years to which the co-owner of the unit being sold is entitled to a portion, in proportion to the percentage interest assigned to his unit in the master deed. Since the co-owner typically cannot seek a refund from the association of his share of the owners' equity, because it is treated as a part of the undivided ownership interest of the co-owner in the unit and common areas, there is no reason why there should be any proration or adjustment of owner's equity in a resale purchase agreement. Rather, the fair market value of the condominium unit purchased should reflect the value of the cubicle of space being sold, the seller's undivided interest in the common areas and the financial condition of the condominium association. The purchaser, therefore, should not allow the broker, who may have drafted the purchase agreement as agent on behalf of the seller, to provide for any type of proration of owner's equity unless the condominium documents specifically authorize the reimbursement of owner's equity to the seller. In that case, there will then be some reasonable basis to prorate the equity between purchaser and seller.

In summary, when looking at condominium units, you should consider the factors discussed in this chapter to help you decide whether you have the "aptitude" to buy a:

• New unit from the developer,

• Conversion unit from the developer,

• Used unit in what was a "new construction" project, or

• Used unit in what was a "conversion" project.

IT'S LIKE FINDING THE RIGHT MATE

Now that you have some idea as to the location in which you desire to purchase, and whether you will consider some, or all, of new, conversion, and resale condominiums, you are ready to locate a real estate broker who has had experience in buying and selling condominium units in the locale in which you are interested. A knowledgeable real estate broker should have insight into the better quality condominiums that are available. He should help you to spot those condominium projects that are better managed, and in which the units have appreciated with regularity. A real estate broker also may know of available new construction and may have some idea of the "track record" of the developer.

You also should check local newspaper advertisements and/or the Internet for condominiums, and you may wish to talk to friends and acquaintances who know of existing condominiums that will soon be on the market. But an additional word of caution! If, after reading this book four times as prescribed, you still have no perception of what condo living is about, you should make an appointment with a condominium attorney who should spend at least an hour answering any questions you may have concerning the condominium concept, and especially whether you are a person who should contemplate buying a condo!

YOU MEAN I WILL OWN THAT, TOO?

Perhaps the most common error of the prospective condominium purchaser is the failure to understand that a purchaser will buy not only the cubicle of space in which he will live, but also an undivided interest in the common elements of the project. Even though the condominium unit under consideration may be the home of his dreams, the intelligent purchaser will appreciate that he ultimately will be responsible for a portion of the costs of maintenance, repair, and/or replacement of all common areas of the condominium for which the condominium association has responsibility. Consequently, his inspection should not be limited to the condominium unit but should encompass the condominium as a whole.

For example, if the roofs of buildings in a distant portion of the condominium project are deteriorating and the condominium documents provide that the association is responsible for the maintenance of the roofs (as is usually the case), the fact that your own roof is in good condition and will not soon leak may not mean that your investment in the condominium project will be a good one. The association may be required to levy substantial special or additional assessments to defray the cost to replace the roofs at the other end of the project. Or, if the roofs were defectively constructed by the developer and the right to sue has not expired, the association may start a lawsuit against the developer, which, potentially, may cost tens of thousands of dollars to prosecute.

THE CONTRACT

The following discussion of Michigan law and practice is for illustration only. Of course, you should check with your condominium lawyer as to the particular statutes and common law of your state regarding pre-construction agreements.

In Michigan, the Condominium Act prescribes many of the rights and responsibilities of a condominium developer. Assuming you have located a "new construction" condominium unit that you want to buy, but which is not yet constructed, you may be asked to sign a reservation agreement.

The typical reservation agreement reserves the particular unit you have selected (assuming that you later elect to go ahead with the transaction), in consideration of which you give the developer a deposit as assurance that you are a serious purchaser. The Condominium Act requires that the deposit be held, generally, by a title company or bank, in escrow, pending your final decision to buy the unit.

Typically, a reservation agreement is binding on neither the developer nor the prospective purchaser. The developer will include various "escape clauses" in the reservation agreement, particularly if the developer decides not to develop the condominium project or to construct the particular unit. Similarly, the purchaser may withdraw from a reservation agreement and recover his deposit at any time before the unit is established in the master deed and the purchaser signs a binding purchase agreement.

BEFORE YOU SIGN

In Michigan, the purchase agreement only becomes binding after the purchaser has been given an opportunity to review the condominium documents that will control the operation and development of the condominium project and have been recorded in the public records of the county where the condominium project is located.

Never sign a binding real estate purchase agreement without first seeking the advice of legal counsel, unless the binding effect of the purchase agreement is expressly contingent upon your attorney's subsequent review and satisfaction with its contents!

Such is certainly true in the context of a condominium. For example, in Michigan, when the developer asks that you replace the non-binding reservation agreement with a binding purchase agreement, the developer also must provide you with a number of additional documents, and the prescribed time in which to review them, before the purchase agreement becomes binding. Those documents which the developer of a Michigan condominium must provide a purchaser include the:

- Master Deed, Condominium Bylaws and Subdivision Plan;

- Articles of Incorporation and Association Bylaws of the non-profit condominium association (the Condominium Bylaws and Association Bylaws may be combined);

- Rules and regulations, if any, of the condominium association that may have been promulgated by the developer;

- Disclosure Statement, a plain-English description of the condominium project prepared by the developer (which will be discussed in greater detail later in this book); and,

- *Condominium Buyers Handbook,* a publication presently published by the Michigan Department of Labor and Economic Growth designed to acquaint readers with some of the basic aspects of condominium living.

Although the *Condominium Buyers Handbook* certainly is no substitute for this book (you may have noticed by now that I have discarded all pretense at humility), it does serve to open the eyes of prospective purchasers to some of the pitfalls and problems in buying a condominium, and should be read thoroughly.

In Michigan, a purchase agreement typically contains such elements as the purchase price, terms, legal description of the unit and condominium project, description of any assigned carports, boat wells, parking spaces, etc., and description of conditions of and remedies after default. There also are certain legally mandated provisions that a developer must include in the purchase agreement when selling a residential condo unit in Michigan. First, the developer must give the purchaser at least nine business days from the date that he receives the Condominium Documents to determine whether he desires to withdraw from the purchase.

This right to withdraw must be set forth in the purchase agreement, although it can be waived by a prospective purchaser. This "cooling-off" period should never be waived unless the purchaser already is fully acquainted with the condominium and condominium documents and is certain he wishes to go ahead with the purchase arrangement. You should, of course, find out whether your own state law provides for a similar cooling-off period, and, if so, determine the time period prescribed.

A Michigan condominium purchase agreement also must contain provisions for the escrow of deposits, notice of the purchaser's exclusive right to arbitrate any dispute between the purchaser and the developer, provided that the amount at issue is less than $2,500, and of the association's exclusive right to arbitrate any dispute between the association and the developer, provided that the amount at issue is less than $10,000.

The State of Michigan no longer regulates the contents of the purchase agreement. Consequently, in Michigan, as in any other state which has "deregulated" its condominium law, a purchaser should have an experienced condominium attorney review the purchase agreement to insure that the developer has complied with the dictates of the statute and that the purchase agreement is otherwise reasonable, enforceable, and properly and clearly sets forth the arrangement that has been struck. At a minimum, a purchase agreement should set forth:

• The unit number you are purchasing;

• The price you are paying;

• Any conditions regarding installment payments on the purchase price;

• Your obligation to pay assessments to the condominium association as well as an initial working capital deposit and perhaps contributions toward the insurance reserve and reserve for major repair and replacement;

• The cancellation rights of the purchaser (usually limited to the period before the agreement becomes binding);

• The cancellation rights, if any, of the developer;

• Warranty provisions and guarantees, if any;

• The "fact" that the purchaser may not rely on oral representations; and,

• Provisions governing the rights and responsibilities of the parties after a default by the purchaser or developer.

You should make a point to ask your condominium developer to commit to the date when your unit will be ready for occupancy, particularly if it has not been constructed. The time when it is available not only profoundly affects when you will be willing to leave your present residence, but also when you will be able to get financing and for how long. Generally, mortgage companies will give commitments for a minimum of 60 days and no longer than six months.

Sometimes the developers and builders of condominiums and single-family homes don't deliver the unit or house as promised. Most developers will give themselves, legally, at least a year to build a condominium unit while holding your funds in escrow. You may or may not be willing to wait that long. And, of course, the purchase agreement will generally exclude delays caused by strikes, acts of God, or other emergencies beyond the control of the developer. Try to get the developer to commit to a "time certain" that is no more than six months from the time that you sign the purchase agreement—unless you are completely flexible about moving into the unit whenever the developer has it ready and if "locking in" an interest rate on a mortgage is not an issue.

In the case of a conversion condominium, the unit should be ready for occupancy unless the developer is undertaking a substantial refurbishing of the condominium project, in which case you should also be concerned about when the unit will be available for occupancy.

The purchase agreement used for the sale of a condominium by a developer may differ substantially from that used in a "resale" situation. In Michigan, a "resale" purchase agreement is not regulated by any statutory provisions that relate specifically to condominiums. Nevertheless, good legal practice dictates that a purchase agreement for a resale condominium contain all customary provisions that define and protect the rights and obligations of the purchaser and seller of residential property (inclusive of a seller's statutory required disclosure statement), generally, and additional provisions unique to the condominium concept, such as:

- Protection for the proration of assessments of condominium units;

- A statement assigning responsibility for additional or special assessments which may be levied;

- Disclosure whether there are any assessments that have been levied but will not be due by the time of closing;

- Provisions for the removal of any contingencies which may be contained in the condominium documents, such as a "right of first refusal" of the condominium association or certain co-owners, or any other restraint on alienation which must be waived; and,

- Assurance that the condominium premises are being sold in a proper and workmanlike condition.

Before signing any purchase agreement, you should consult with your prospective lender as to the length of any commitment it will give you. You may also wish to ask your real estate agent or the developer about the availability of financing for the condominium unit that you are considering. Sometimes a developer will arrange better-than-market-rate mortgages with a local financial institution, based on the volume of units to be sold or because the developer has "bought down" the mortgage, that is, reduced the interest rate or points required to be paid.

The disclosure statement required by the Michigan Condominium Act to be prepared by the developer is an extremely valuable tool for review by the purchaser and his legal counsel. A developer is required in the disclosure statement to disclose material information about the development of the condominium project, relevant information concerning the operation of the association, and the history and background of the developer.

The disclosure statement, which is vaguely akin to a prospectus for a new stock offering, must include:

• The nature of the units constructed or proposed to be constructed;

• How large the condominium project may become;

• How long the developer has to enlarge or contract the project;

• Whether recreational facilities have to be constructed and, if so, under what conditions;

• The identity of the developer and, if a corporation, joint venture, partnership, etc., the identity of its principals;

• Whether the developer has had any prior experience in developing condominiums and, if so, where and when;

• Whether there are any pending legal and/or administrative proceedings against the developer that relate to the project;

• What will be expected of the purchaser in regard to his responsibilities as a co-owner (including a brief summary of the restrictions attributable to the condominium project);

• Whether the roads and sewers of the condominium project will be private or public, and

• Any "other unique and/or material aspects of the condominium project that should be disclosed to prospective purchasers," such as warranties or any disclaimer of warranties.

There usually will be attached to the disclosure statement a copy of a proposed budget for the condominium association, which should give the prospective purchaser an inkling of what he will have to pay in assessments to the condominium association.

Careful scrutiny of the budget frequently will result in the conclusion that the budget has been understated, or that it is based upon units in the condominium project that have not, as yet, been established, or may never be established in the exercise of the developer's discretion in expanding the project.

The developer may intentionally underestimate the actual cost to operate the association; remember, a high "maintenance fee" may be an impediment to sales. This practice is referred to as "low-balling" and, unfortunately, historically was a serious problem in the sale of condominium units. With the increased disclosure requirements of the so-called "second-generation" state statutes, developers now can be more readily held accountable for any intentional misrepresentation of the financial ability of the association to satisfy its needs, as reflected in the anticipated budget prepared by the developer.

Keep in mind that the disclosure statement must be updated periodically by the developer. When you are contemplating buying a condominium unit, you should ask the developer whether this is the latest disclosure statement, when it was prepared, and whether there have been any material changes of the facts set forth in the disclosure statement. You may even wish to have the developer confirm that fact in writing.

Also keep in mind that the disclosure statement will include disclaimers of oral representations made by the developer and/or its sales agents. A bright "red flag" should appear before your eyes whenever a sales representative tells you that you should not worry about any statement set forth in the purchase agreement or condominium documents!

While the law may give you some support, if you intend to rely upon oral representations that contradict the express terms of the purchase agreement or any of the condominium documents, those statements should be reduced to writing before you sign the purchase agreement.

The developer also may disclose in its disclosure statement the form of management under which the condominium association will operate. Consider whether the association is being managed by a professional management company and, if so, whether the professional management company is a subsidiary of the developer or whether it is an outside management company that has no direct affiliation with the developer.

The significance of whether the developer is the managing agent of the condominium association may have some bearing on whether the developer has had prior experience in managing condominiums and whether the developer is sincere in trying to establish a condominium association which will be well-run, not only in its initial stages, but also after the association has been turned over to the co-owners.

In short, the disclosure statement can be a valuable source of information to you and your attorney. It can serve as a source reference to gain additional insight and information about the developer's present and future plans for the condominium project and its experiences in past condominiums.

If the developer discloses the names of condominiums that it has developed or with which it has been affiliated, if it has had such experience, you or your attorney should inquire of the officers, directors, and managing agents of those associations as to the experiences they have had with the developer.

In a resale condo, your state may have a separate "seller disclosure statement" requirement that applies generally to any residential resale situation, and requires disclosure of any common element problems, such as in Michigan.

Simply stated, the more you know about the developer before you buy, the more enlightened your purchase will be. That will be a recurring theme in this book, and you will be glad that you remembered it if you buy a condominium unit.

CHAPTER 4 | Location, Location, Location
Purchasing a Condo as an Investment

In a sense, everyone who buys a condominium or any other real estate is making an investment. While the primary purpose may be to find a suitable place to live, the purchaser normally expects or, at least, formerly expected, that his home will appreciate, at a minimum, at the current rate of inflation. A condominium also can be purchased as an investment, without the expectation that it will be occupied as one's primary residence. This chapter will focus on the various types of condominiums and consider, briefly, which can be considered a potentially good investment.

SECOND HOME VS. INVESTMENT PROPERTY

We'll first discuss purchasing a condo as a second home, either as a pure investment or as an outlet for recreational activities.

Regardless of tax ramifications, from a purely financial standpoint, a condominium as a recreational or second home may be a good investment, depending on the location of the condominium, its proximity to the investor, the facilities offered, and the like. The cash flow generated by a condominium, which is not used as the primary home of the investor, frequently does not meet the actual expenses incurred in operating and maintaining the condominium, including debt service, assessments, and taxes, insurance, and rental management fees. However, when appreciation and certain favorable tax advantages also are considered, investment in a residential condo may well prove beneficial.

Second home condos have been extremely popular in certain areas of the country. Florida, for example, has seen the greatest development of condos as second homes. Many owners of Florida condos are residents of other states, particularly in the Northeast and Midwest. A "second home" condominium in Florida, California, Colorado, or another so-called "prime" recreational location may be a good investment, but the investor should use good common sense and adhere to the criteria outlined in other places in this book.

THE COMMERCIAL CONDOMINIUM

The potential of the commercial condominium is only now being recognized. Initially, the commercial condominium seems to have found its greatest acceptance in Southern California, but appear throughout the country.

Commercial condominiums may take the form of office buildings, warehouses, parking structures, industrial parks, or storage facilities. They make economic sense to the investor—usually a corporation, limited partnership, or limited liability company—that does not find it appropriate to pay rent and expects to benefit from the potential for appreciation in value.

A potential problem for the investor in a commercial condominium is the limitation that is inherently imposed on it regarding the space purchased. For example, the doctor who buys an office suite in a commercial condominium may later run out of space and be unable to expand—unless there are convertible areas or he has reserved the right to buy additional space from the condominium developer, the association, or other co-owners in the project. The investor who makes a wrong business decision may experience that "boxed in" feeling! The commercial condominium can be an excellent investment opportunity for the right investor. On the other hand, it is always easier to walk away when one's property is rented rather than owned.

Many state condominium statutes impose fewer restrictions on a commercial condominium than on a residential condominium. One should check the particular state involved to determine the requirements imposed upon the developer and the condominium association concerning the creation, operation, and management of the commercial condominium project.

Commercial condominiums do share some of the same risks as residential condominiums. Proper management, as well as a spirit of community participation and cooperation, is indispensable. In the commercial condominium, an investor should examine the documents of the project to determine if they provide adequate flexibility to meet the future needs of the potential co-owner or tenant. Flexibility should exist for the expansion or contraction of the size of the condominium unit purchased, the maintenance of common facilities, and the division of the costs of operation of the condominium association, particularly if it is a mixed-use development, i.e., commercial and residential.

MOBILE HOME CONDOMINIUMS

Although it may be financially more lucrative for the experienced mobile home operator to retain ownership and lease the pads, both the inexperienced operator and the operator who wishes to avoid the day-to-day landlord/tenant aspects of the mobile home community (while retaining, where appropriate and legal, the right to manage the mobile home park for the benefit of the mobile home condominium association) may wish to consider the development and sale of mobile home condominium communities, or the conversion of existing mobile home parks to condominium. The "economics" will dictate whether such an investment is feasible. As with all real estate investments, the most important factor always is "location, location, location."

With the benefit of careful drafting of the mobile home community documents, the mobile home community can be a viable place in which to live and/or invest. The condominium documents should give the condominium association the latitude and powers necessary to effectively address the unique problems of the mobile home community.

The conversion mobile home condominium has not been widely accepted. The market for mobile homes is composed primarily of lower income individuals who lack sufficient equity to invest in a typical residential community. Similarly, the inherently "transient" nature of the mobile home occupant may make management by a mobile home condominium association more difficult than management by a mobile home operator who may simply evict the tenant who violates the rules and regulations. Finally, the multiplicity of regulations governing the sale of mobile homes is likely to be a deterrent to conversion. Consider also that many state condominium statutes contain provisions that are unique to mobile home condominiums. In Michigan, for example, the developer of a mobile home condominium can sell individual mobile home lots, together with an undivided interest in a community facility.

CAMPSITE CONDOMINIUMS

As with the mobile home condominium, the campsite condo involves the purchase of a plot of land, or envelope of space, within a campsite community, sometimes containing electrical hookups for recreational vehicles within the unit. Typically, ownership of a "campsite" may include a recreational facility, which offers recreational equipment complementary to campsite use. Again, depending on the location and price of the campsite facility, an investment in a campsite condominium may be beneficial, particularly when the investor contemplates permanent and frequent personal use. However, one should carefully evaluate the availability of, and the responsibility to obtain and maintain, water, utilities, and improvements and whether they are yearlong.

There are unique problems to campsite condos that must be addressed in the condominium documents. The demarcation of the site from a physical standpoint may pose problems—not only for the developer but also for the purchaser. Adequate maintenance and management of the campsite condo is also extremely important. Finally, although the adequacy of restrictions on the leasing of sites may be a problem in any residential community, this appears to be particularly true in the context of campsite and mobile home parks.

MIXED USE, RETAIL, AND HOTEL CONDOMINIUMS

Mixed-use condominiums are growing rapidly in popularity, particularly in urban locations. The mixed-use condo typically is a high-rise building that may include retail and entertainment space, commercial office space, and residential apartments. The availability of retail and entertainment services in immediate proximity to one's residence may be particularly attractive to the young, single, urban professional, who may enhance his or her ability to balance the time demands of work, play, and home. Similarly, the developer of a mixed-use condominium who has no interest in the traditional leasing business may find that the mixed-use retail residential condominium enhances the value of all components of his project.

It is hard to imagine a retailer buying retail condominium space in an office building or "strip" center without first ascertaining the desirability of the project and location. A retail condominium may be a sensible investment if the business location is independently attractive and the customer base enhanced by the proximity of residential condominium occupants. When these conditions are satisfied, the retailer's ability to avoid the payment of rent and to share in the presumed appreciation of the project will constitute the "icing on the cake."

As has been previously discussed in the commercial condominium context, the needs of the retail purchaser may change, either downward or upward. The retailer must recognize that the marketability of condominium space may be inferior to the marketability of rental space. The investor may be "locked in" to the purchased retail space without the ability to reduce his fixed costs, or alternatively, may be unable to expand to meet new needs or opportunities—in either case to the detriment of his business.

HOTELS

Hotel condominiums generally are found in portions of the country that attract vacationers. Miami Beach and Florida in general are havens for hotel condominiums. Many hotel condominiums are offered as "time-share" condos, whereby the investor actually purchases the right to use a hotel room or suite and the associated hotel facilities for a fixed number of weeks or days during the year.

From an investment standpoint, a developer who buys a hotel and converts it into a hotel or time-share condominium can, dependent upon the usual factors of location and price, obtain an excellent return on his investment. Time-share condos could take an entire chapter of this book. Suffice it to say that time-sharing has been abused by many developers, and many purchasers fail to understand the actual concept of buying into a time-share condominium (or time shares of any kind).

Simply stated, a hotel or time-share condominium will be a risky investment if the investor is not prepared to use the condo on a frequent basis, or if the investor fails to ensure that the leasing of the hotel condo throughout the year is viable and makes economic sense. If possible, the investor should invest in a hotel or time-share condo that offers the option to exchange the room with similar rooms in hotels located in other parts of the world.

As with any other type of used real estate, the purchaser must be aware of the physical condition of the premises prior to purchase. The developer should be prepared to adequately disclose the condition of the premises and make the necessary renovations to put the converted condominium hotel in proper condition.

The developer of a hotel condominium should be advised of the legal and business consequences of doing so and should retain the services of a lawyer with expertise in the sub-specialty of condominium hotel development. Moreover, the prospective purchaser of a hotel or time-share condominium interest should closely examine the condominium documents before investing.

PARKING LOT CONDOMINIUMS

The parking lot condominium is well suited to the sports fan who purchases season tickets for his favorite team each year and wishes to park close to the stadium. Simply stated, the investor in a parking lot condo buys a premium parking lot space near an office complex or recreational or sports facility. While parking lot condos are relatively new, I believe they will be highly successful, particularly since parking spaces in major downtown communities around the country are limited and their rental extremely expensive. This would appear to be an area of considerable opportunity for the condominium investor. But, again, the management of the parking facility and enforcement of its restrictions are extremely important components for success.

MARINA CONDOMINIUMS

Marina condominiums are well established as an investment opportunity. As with parking lots, boat slips are hard to find in prime locations. The condominium marina developer may realize an excellent investment return by selling the boat slips but maintaining the management responsibilities (when permitted by local law) and/or services to the marina.

A marina condominium investment can be lucrative for the boat owner, or even for the person who expects to buy a boat at some later time but desires to rent his boat slip in the interim. The investor who buys a marina boat slip does not have to worry that one may not be available for his boat. Moreover, the value of the boat slip is likely to appreciate because of the scarcity of prime boat slip locations and facilities.

This is not to say that marina condominiums are without problems. The boat slip condominium developer must obtain the proper clearances from federal and state agencies and otherwise comply with state and federal laws regarding the division of water rights. The proper engineering of seawalls and "catwalks" should be confirmed, and not assumed, by the prospective purchaser. As with all condominiums, the documentation for the marina condominium should be properly prepared and the purchase price reasonable.

In summary, condominiums take various forms, and inventive developers and their attorneys are likely to devise new and ingenious uses of the condominium concept in the future. The condominium offers a viable alternative to leasing for those who would prefer to own, rather than rent, real estate. Perhaps soon there will be condominiums in outer space or under water (by design). Perhaps future space transports will contain a retail condominium like shops do today. In any event, the opportunities for condominium investment and development are limited only by state and federal laws and the imagination of man.

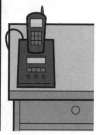

CHAPTER **5** | The Best of Both Worlds
Vacation Homes and Taxes

Our review of the condominium as an investment would be incomplete if I failed to mention the tax ramifications. Of particular significance is the so-called "vacation condominium," which typically is a condo used as a secondary residence or investment, not for homestead occupancy.

The treatment of vacation condominiums under the Internal Revenue Code is similar to the treatment afforded a house, apartment, mobile home, boat, or similar property. There are specific limitations on the allowable business deductions available to a taxpayer who uses a vacation home for both personal and rental purposes. These limitations apply to individuals, S-corporations, partnerships, trusts, and estates. The number of days that a vacation home is used for personal purposes, as compared to the number of days that the property is rented at fair market value, determines the availability of tax deductions.

As of the date of publication the second edition of this book, these rules may be summarized as follows:

- Rule No. 1: If the vacation condominium is used by the taxpayer for personal purposes for not more than fourteen (14) days during the taxable year, or for ten percent (10%) of the number of days that it is rented at a fair price (if this is greater), then it is not considered the taxpayer's "home." In this case, tax deductions attributable to income derived from the rental of the property are not limited to gross income produced by the property.

- Rule No. 2: If the personal use of the vacation condominium exceeds the greater of: (a) fourteen (14) days; or (b) ten percent (10%) of the number of days during the taxable year that it is rented at a fair price, then it is considered the taxpayer's "home." In such cases, the tax deductions attributable to income derived from the rental of the property cannot exceed the gross income generated by the property.

- Rule No. 3: If the vacation condominium is the taxpayer's "home" and is rented for fewer than fifteen (15) days during the tax year, any income derived from the rental during the tax year is not taxable, but the deductions attributable to income derived from the rental of the property are not allowed (the usual and allowable personal deductions for mortgage, interest, and real estate taxes, however, may be taken).

- Rule No. 4: If the vacation condominium is not the taxpayer's "home," as described under the vacation home rules, but the rental use is not an activity from which the taxpayer expects to make a profit, the taxpayer's deductible rental expenses may not exceed his rental income, in the same manner as they are limited for a "home" under the vacation home rules. However, if the rental results in a profit during three (3) or more years during a period of five (5) consecutive tax years, it is presumed by the IRS to be an activity engaged in "for profit."

In all cases, except the situation described in Rule No. 3, the personal use of the vacation property, on even a single day, requires that investment expenses be allocated between personal and rental use based on the number of personal days and the number of rental days. The allocation between personal and rental expense is calculated, usually, in the following ratio:

Days rented at a fair rental price
Days of total use

According to the IRS, "days of total use" equals the number of days the property was rented at a fair rental price plus the number of days of personal use. "Days rented at a fair rental price" is the number of days the property was rented at a fair rental price, excluding any day that the taxpayer also personally used the home. Days that the vacation home is vacant (even if the home is being advertised for rent at a fair rental value) and days spent maintaining the home are not included as days of personal use.

What constitutes "personal use"? The taxpayer is deemed to have used his vacation home for "personal use" for the entire day, even if it is used for only a part of that day, in any of the following instances:

1. If the taxpayer, a member of his family or any person who has an interest in the home uses it for any part of the day, it is a "personal use" day. Family includes the spouse, brothers, sisters, lineal descendants, and ancestors of the taxpayer. However, if the family member rents the vacation property for a fair price for use as his principal residence on that day, this use is

not considered "personal use" by the taxpayer. However, if the taxpayer stays at the home while renting it to a family member who is using it as a principal residence, the days that the taxpayer spends at the vacation home count as days of "personal use" by the taxpayer, regardless of the rental agreement.

2. If the vacation home is used by an individual under an arrangement that enables the taxpayer to use some other unit (whether or not fair rental is charged for the use of the other house), the taxpayer is considered to have used the vacation home for "personal use." Thus, a house-swapping arrangement, under which two homeowners rent each other's home as a personal residence, is "personal use" by each taxpayer.

3. Unless a fair rental is received, any period of rental of a vacation home is considered to be "personal use" by the taxpayer.

It generally is to the taxpayer's advantage to avoid having a dwelling unit classified as his "home," because it would subject rental deductions to the gross rent loss limitation. Therefore, most tax planning strategies involve controlling the variables of the fixed formula: rental days and personal days.

Unless an individual rents a unit for fewer than fifteen (15) days, he or she would be wise to rent it at a fair rental price for as many days as possible (assuming a rental loss) since doing so will increase the number of personal use days a taxpayer can have before the loss limitation applies. To avoid having a vacation condominium classified as the taxpayer's "home," he should carefully plan the number of days it is used for personal purposes during the tax year. The fewer the number of personal use days, the less likely the chance that the vacation condominium can be classified as the taxpayer's "home."

In summary, if a vacation condominium is used solely by the owner for personal purposes, the mortgage interest and taxes are

allocable as itemized deductions, but other expenses, such as utilities, repairs, depreciation, and rent paid on the home cannot, in
most instances, be deducted. The tax ramifications of a vacation
home bought strictly as a business investment are equally un-
complicated. When an individual enters into a business venture
for the sole purpose of producing income, these deductions are
allowed (for example, a rental property leased to others at a fair
rent is eligible for tax deductions). When a dwelling unit is used
for both personal and business purposes, mortgage interest and
taxes will still be deductible and the rules, while more complex,
may still permit the deduction of other expenses, to the extent
allocated to the days rented. An understanding of these rules can
aid taxpayers in making prudent tax decisions regarding vacation homes. You are advised to seek advice from a competent tax
consultant of your choice before making any purchase, and to
confirm the validity of these comments of the tax law, when you
are about to proceed, to insure that they are still applicable.

CHAPTER 6 | **Closing Time**
Guidelines for Selling a Condo

Initially following their introduction in the 1960s, the market for the resale of condominiums was a seesaw affair. There was the difficulty in recognizing condominiums as a viable form of ownership appropriate for the investor, including the person who wished to live in the condominium as his primary residence.

In the 1960s and 1970s, condominiums were the "new kid on the block." Most financial institutions were skeptical of them. Add to that scenario the horror stories from Florida, where unscrupulous developer abuses included the "low-balling" of assessments, shoddy workmanship, and inequitable recreational leases. As a result, there developed a general disdain for condominiums in many parts of the country.

With the passage of time, condominiums gained acceptance

and are now not only accepted but are glamorized by Hollywood. John Paxton wrote a song about condos and yuppies. Condos for the vacation home-rental market have flourished in Ft. Lauderdale, Aspen, Naples, Dana Point, Palm Beach, and South Beach. High-rise condos are a hot item, particularly in New York, Chicago, Washington D.C. and Singapore.

SELLING GUIDELINES

In this chapter, we will consider guidelines for the seller of a residential condominium. We will assume that the person selling the condominium is not desperate to do so, notwithstanding that he may have served on the board of directors, may have contracted "condominium depression" or may have been persecuted by the condominium association. We also will assume that he is not motivated to sell by his refusal to adhere to rules and regulations or because he has been embarrassed by the condo association in its efforts to compel compliance with the condominium documents. Moreover, we will assume that he is not desperate to sell because the condominium association has failed to fix his roof, but rather he has, both literally and figuratively, "thrown in the towel."

We are, rather, assuming that the co-owner is selling his unit for a reason having nothing to do with the condominium itself, is willing to comply with the requirements of state law and the condominium documents when selling the unit, and will exercise sound judgment and business practices in his effort to obtain the best price for the unit.

When a person sells a condominium unit, he must first determine how he will list the unit for sale. Many condominium documents prohibit the posting of signs concerning the sale of a condominium unit. You should check with your condominium association to determine its current policy, if any, in that respect. Such restrictions may impair your ability to sell "By Owner."

If the association does allow the placement of a "for sale" sign in a window or elsewhere in his unit, the Realtor or the seller may choose to use that opportunity. A word to the wise: If signs are not allowed and your lawyer advises you, based on the facts that you have provided him, that the prohibition against "for sale" signs is enforceable, you should follow the dictates of the condominium documents and not have the sign posted in your condominium.

Remember, however, that even if signs are permitted, you may benefit from the assistance of a professional real estate broker in selling your unit. In all probability, a professional real estate broker will have access to one or more "multi-list" capabilities. Moreover, although he or she probably will not be an attorney, a professional real estate broker is likely to be knowledgeable concerning real estate title and closing document issues.

If the seller desires to engage a real estate professional, he should check with other people in the project to obtain the names of brokers who have been successful in selling condominiums at the project, who have established a rapport with the board of directors or its management company, and who otherwise understand the obligations of the real estate broker and the seller concerning condominium documents and the state statutes regarding the sale of a unit. He should be careful not to pick a real estate broker who lacks knowledge of condominiums, since, if he does so, he may sell the condominium but buy a lawsuit from his purchaser or condominium association, based on his failure to comply with the law or the condominium documents.

The seller does not want a real estate person who will make false or misleading statements to the purchaser concerning condominium living or what the purchaser can do at that condominium. Doing so will cause problems for both the real estate broker and seller.

The seller, in his listing agreement with the broker, should have a provision that the broker has no authority to make representations concerning the condition and nature of the premises except as expressly set forth in the Listing Agreement or the Purchase Agreement. By doing so, the seller helps to insulate himself from potential liability for misrepresentations by the broker.

Regardless of whether the seller engages a real estate broker, the seller should consider employing an attorney to advise him concerning his responsibilities as seller. A developing body of statutory and case law holds that sellers and/or their sales representatives must disclose all known or readily determinable facts which the purchaser would consider material to his decision to purchase, including, without limitation, facts concerning defects and deficiencies in the condominium unit. It is likely that the required disclosures apply both to the unit being sold (that is, typically, the cubicle of space the seller owns outright in the traditional condominium) and, if known, to the nature and condition of the "common elements."

The seller may wish to confirm with the board of directors the status of any assessments that are due and owing on his unit, and to determine whether the board intends to levy any special assessments in the near future. If a special assessment has been levied and is payable in installments, the seller should advise his attorney of that fact so arrangements for the proration of that assessment may be made in the purchase agreement.

Once the seller has decided whether he wishes to hire a professional real estate broker and/or has engaged a qualified attorney, he should notify the condominium association, if required by the condominium documents, of his intent to sell the unit. There may be another advantage to doing so, since many associations maintain a list of prospective purchasers or an in-house real estate person to help co-owners sell units. The seller also should verify that the association has complied with FNMA-FHLMC and other secondary mortgage lender requirements that will be important to a purchaser when he seeks financing. (If the association has not obtained FHA, FNMA, or FHLMC approval, for example, it should strive to become certified by FHA.) Finally, the seller should indicate in the purchase agreement that the assessments of the association may increase substantially and that the seller has no direct control over the nature and extent of the assessment being levied by the condominium association. Of course, if the seller is presently on the board of directors, then an additional disclaimer should be included regarding his activities as a director of the association, that is, to the effect that he assumes no responsibilities regarding the operation of the association to the purchaser.

"AS IS, WHERE IS"

If there are any defects or deficiencies in his unit that the seller knows, or suspects, exist, he should get an inspection report and provide it to a prospective purchaser, together with an adequate disclaimer in bold print that the purchaser is buying the condominium unit in "as is" condition, without express or implied warranties, guaranties, or representations of any type.

The purchaser should be encouraged to obtain his own inspection report, if necessary, and the purchase agreement should reflect that advice. Similarly, the seller should clearly indicate that the common elements of the condominium project are not guaranteed in any way, and that the purchaser is obligated to and acknowledges that he has inspected (or has had adequate opportunity to make his own investigation of) the condition of the common elements, and that he is buying the same as part of his unit on an "as is, where is" basis, without express or implied warranties, guaranties, or representations of any type as to their condition, composition, or nature.

Many condominium projects, particularly the older ones, contain a "right of first refusal" that gives the association the right to buy your unit on the same terms and conditions as that of a bona fide prospective purchaser. If a purchaser is found, you should comply with any "right of first refusal" that the condominium documents provide to the association.

"Rights of first refusal" are rarely exercised and are rarely found in the condominium documents of newer condominiums, particularly because VA, FHA, and other secondary mortgage lenders prohibit such provisions because of their susceptibility to abuse. Rights of first refusal have always been subject to the claim that their threatened exercise is merely a subterfuge for the board of directors to discriminate on the basis of race, color, creed, religion, national origin, etc. They cannot lawfully be used for discriminatory purposes.

Nevertheless, the right of first refusal has been upheld by courts if the association follows criteria that do not relate to legally prohibited classifications but instead are based on sound economic principles. For example, it would be improper for an association to exercise its right of first refusal with the intention to keep a couple of a particular race from buying a unit in the condominium, but it would be reasonable for that association to exclude a person with a notoriously bad credit rating.

In many states, the condominium documents may contain reasonable restrictions on the sale and leasing of units. Not infrequently, these restrictions limit the number of units that may be leased in order to comply with requirements of the secondary mortgage market. More frequently, the seller must provide the condominium association with the details of sale. Such details may include the name of the purchaser, the terms and conditions of purchase, the name of the mortgage company, and a certification that the purchaser has received a complete set of the condominium documents and acknowledges his willingness and obligation to comply with them. The association may have recourse against the seller if he fails to comply with this covenant.

It is in the seller's best interest to cooperate with the condominium association to avoid problems that may arise if the association has rights that were not exercised because it did not have actual knowledge of the sale. Moreover, the seller will wish to avoid causing problems for the purchaser with the association since the purchaser will, no doubt, seek recourse against the seller for his failure to comply with the obligations of the condominium documents. Of course, the purchaser should not be naive as to the seller's obligations and may wish to be assured that the seller has complied with all obligations of the condominium documents and relevant state statutes regarding the sale of the unit.

Assuming that the prerequisites of the condominium documents have been satisfied by the giving of notice to the condominium association, and that the sale is to be consummated, the seller should take the same precautions concerning the purchase agreement as he would in the sale of any other type of residential or commercial property. The purchase agreement should be in writing, spelling out, among other things, the basis by which all prorations of taxes, condominium assessments, both regular and special, and any reserve or working capital deposits will be made. Perhaps the most common mistake made by the seller or purchaser of residential real estate of any kind is the assumption that the purchase agreement is a formality, and that legal advice is not needed until the transaction is closed (if then). Nothing could be further from the truth. Too often, the attorney's hands are tied by the time he is first consulted!

THE REAL ESTATE CLOSING

Once a purchase agreement has been drafted and reviewed by legal counsel (preferably, before it becomes binding), the seller should assist his real estate broker and/or attorney to obtain and provide to the purchaser the information necessary to satisfy any conditions to the purchase agreement becoming binding. For instance, it will be necessary to provide the purchaser with a complete set of the condominium documents—including any updates and/or amendments—together with the current rules and regulations of the condominium association, if any. Doing this in a timely fashion will also avoid any questions later as to whether the purchaser had actual notice of his obligations as a co-owner under the condominium documents.

If the seller has previously obtained permission from the association to make modifications, either permanent or temporary, to the common elements, those approvals should be disclosed to the purchaser prior to the execution of a purchase agreement (particularly if the approval is temporary). And if the modifications were only temporary, the seller should prepare to remove the modification. (The prudent condominium association, if it allowed modifications but imposed liability on the seller for continual maintenance, repair or replacement responsibility for the modifications, will have had an agreement prepared, executed and recorded in the land title records so that any new purchaser is on constructive notice of those responsibilities, i.e., our firm's "Modification Agreement.")

If the seller has not already done so, the seller also will have to provide at this time whatever information he is required by state statutory or common law to provide to his purchaser concerning his knowledge of defects or deficiencies in the condominium unit. If the condominium unit was constructed prior to 1978, federal law also will require the disclosure of information concerning the presence or absence of lead paint. If the unit is being rented, the seller should provide the purchaser with a copy of the lease, assuming that he has not already done so.

Having provided the purchaser with the condominium documents and other necessary information, the seller should prepare for the closing of the unit with his real estate agent and/or attorney. Part of the obligation of the seller is to insure that the assessments have been paid up to date. The purchaser should protect his interests by requesting a letter from the condominium association indicating how much, if any, is owed to the condominium association for assessments. In Michigan, for example, this request must be made at least five (5) days before closing. The seller, if he is living in the unit, should prepare to move and should make sure he is leaving all items he is obligated by the purchase agreement to leave in the unit.

If the seller is leasing the unit and the purchaser intends to occupy the unit at closing, or shortly thereafter, the seller and purchaser should ensure that there will not be a problem in obtaining possession of the premises from the tenant(s). The seller should have looked at the lease arrangement to determine what rights he has against the tenant. Unless the lease will be assumed by the purchaser, he should make arrangements with the tenant to vacate the premises by a date certain. The seller should be careful, however, that he has left enough time to obtain possession of the premises from his tenant before the closing of the unit or the time when he must surrender possession to the purchaser.

The horror story that sometimes manifests itself is the tenant of the seller who refuses to vacate the premises on time. (The same situation may arise when the seller is unable to move into his new residence and consequently refuses to leave the old.) The purchaser then sues the seller for breach of contract because the seller has failed to deliver possession on the date promised. The purchaser should have a penalty clause in the purchase agreement that provides adequate compensation if the purchaser is not given possession on the date promised, whether or not the seller is in possession of the premises. Conversely, the seller will try to negotiate adequate flexibility in the date of possession to ensure that he can deliver possession to the purchaser when he is required to do so. The seller should attempt to resist penalty clauses concerning the date of possession if he can negotiate around it.

By the date of closing, the prudent seller should have reviewed the closing documents with his attorney and real estate person to ensure that they are in order. In the case of a condominium, it is absolutely imperative that the correct unit description and appurtenances, such as the garage or carport if separately delineated, are conveyed by the warranty deed of conveyance. The seller should be obligated, under most circumstances, to provide a title insurance policy in the amount of the purchase price to the purchaser. The seller should ensure, and a competent title company will require, that the seller provide an affidavit that he has paid off all contractors and suppliers who have performed work on the premises within a certain period before the date of closing to ensure that there are not, and will not, be any liens later recorded against the unit.

Again, it is important that the seller "take care of business" before closing to provide time to cure any problems which may be identified. The seller should invite the purchaser to inspect the unit shortly before closing, and should request that he sign an acknowledgment that the condition of the unit at closing is satisfactory and is in accordance with the purchase agreement, that is, the same as it was when the purchaser first examined the unit before the purchase agreement was signed.

The prudent seller will make available to the purchaser at closing the necessary keys and information concerning the operation of various utilities, etc., serving the condominium unit, and should otherwise be as cooperative as possible. The seller should notify the condominium association that the closing has taken place and vacate the premises in a timely manner.

If all the above items are accomplished, the sale of a unit should be smooth and uneventful. The co-owner will have sold his condominium unit to a purchaser who is knowledgeable about his responsibilities as a purchaser of the condominium, and the condominium association will be satisfied that the seller has complied with his obligations under the condominium documents and has made reasonable efforts to apprise the purchaser of his obligations. The real estate broker will have created good will with the association because he followed the dictates of the condominium documents and policies of the association.

Many of my recommendations regarding the sale of a condominium hold true for the sale of any type of residential housing.

What makes the sale of a condominium unit complex and unique is the imposition of the rights of the condominium association and the condominium documents upon the sales transaction. With the assistance of prudent, competent counsel and a knowledgeable real estate person, the sale of a condominium unit can be a non-event. The purchase price obtained by the seller will relate directly, in most instances, to the manner in which the unit has been maintained and the viability of the project and condominium association as a whole. It is fair to say that a well-run project and condominium association enhance the marketability of all condominium units. It is also fair to say that the seller who adheres to my recommendations will, more than likely, avoid future problems arising from the sale of his condominium unit.

TAX RAMIFICATIONS

You should have considered the tax ramifications of selling your condominium unit before you signed a purchase agreement. Regardless, having successfully unloaded your unit without legal liabilities and entanglements, the Internal Revenue Service will now give you no choice but to do so.

Although this book is not intended as a tax treatise on the ramifications of real estate disposition, it is important to highlight some of the salient sections that may interest the average lay person considering buying or selling a condominium. Although I do not profess to have any particular expertise in tax matters, and this book is not designed to be a substitute for sound advice from a tax attorney or accountant, it may be helpful to understand some of the general tenets applicable to the transfer of real estate as of the publication of this book.

The rules governing the sale of one's principal residence are now contained in Section 121 of the Internal Revenue Code and summarized in IRS Publication 523. In general, a taxpayer may exclude from gross income up to $250,000 in capital gain ($500,000 in the case of a married taxpayer filing jointly, assuming that both husband and wife qualify) realized from the sale of his "main home" if both the "ownership" and "use" tests also are satisfied. (Note that this is an exclusion, not merely a deferral, of capital gain.) There are no longer any limitations upon the number of times that the exclusion may be utilized, assuming that the "main home," ownership, and use tests are met in each case, but the taxpayer must not have excluded gain from the sale of another home within the two (2) year period preceding the current sale.

Publication 523 states that a "main home" may be a house, houseboat, mobile home, cooperative apartment, or condominium. Generally, your main home is the one you live in most of the time. Consequently, it is the position of the Internal Revenue Service that a person whose main home is a property he rents will not qualify for the exclusion. If you have more than one home, you can only exclude gain from the sale of your main home. The usual capital gain rules will apply to the sale of the other home(s) unless they will qualify as property held for business or investment purposes.

The ownership test requires that the taxpayer have owned the home for at least two (2) years during the five (5) year period ending on the date of sale. The use test requires that the taxpayer has lived in the home as his or her main home for at least two (2) years during the same five (5) year period. Short absences, such as for a summer vacation, count as periods of use, but longer absences, such as a one (1) year sabbatical, do not.

The reader should note that the ownership and use periods need not be concurrent, so a taxpayer who rents and lives in the home during, say, years one and two of the five-year period, and then purchases and rents the property for the remainder of the period, might qualify to exclude the gain.

Finally, IRS regulations may recognize a partial exclusion when the taxpayer fails to satisfy either the ownership or use test due to a change in place of employment, health status, or unforeseen circumstances, which are defined to include, among others, death, divorce or legal separation, multiple births, or a change in employment that requires relocation.

Although capital gain from the sale of one's main home may now be excluded up to the amount of the limitations described above, the rules remain complex, particularly if the taxpayer has multiple homes or the main home has been used for both residential and business or investment purposes during the five (5) year period preceding sale. Consequently, I recommend that a tax professional be consulted on all tax related issues.

Now, any good trouper should know about Section 1031, which permits the tax-free exchange of "like-kind" property held for an investment purpose, or for use in a trade or business, for those of you who are treating your condominium as an investment or as business property.

Exchanges of investment and business property have never achieved wide popularity in much of the nation. This is partly because setting up a successful exchange often takes much more patience and homework than arranging a straight purchase and sale of property. Most brokers and investors simply do not understand the potentials of the exchange, or are frightened off by the intricate footwork that sometimes must take place to comply with the strict requirements imposed by the Internal Revenue Code.

The key advantage of the Section 1031 tax-free exchange is that the gain which otherwise would be realized need not be recognized at that time (i.e., tax may not be required to be paid on the gain at the time of sale), except that gain (but not a loss) must be recognized to the extent that money or property which is not like-kind property is received. With that exception, the tax is postponed until a reachable tax disposition occurs on the newly received property. The advantage of this tax postponement is obvious. A series of "exchanges" may permit the deferral of tax recognition indefinitely, and if the property ends up in the estate of the exchanger with a stepped-up basis, tax may be avoided permanently.

Beside the tax advantages, an exchange (whether tax-free or not) can be used as a financing tool, since it permits the substitution of real estate for cash. The investor can reinvest his full capital in new properties without diminution due to tax payments. Uncle Sam, in effect, extends an interest-free loan to the investor, who may leverage his investment to a degree beyond that which may be obtained through mortgage financing.

With the described exception, Section 1031 (a) of the Internal Revenue Code provides that no gain or loss on an exchange of real estate is recognized on property held for productive use in a trade or business, or held for investment, if exchanged solely for property of a like kind which is to be held for productive use in a trade or business, or held as an investment.

Note that the exchange qualifies for tax-free treatment as long as each of the properties involved in the exchange is either property held for productive use in a trade or business or is property held for investment. Thus, property held for productive use in a trade or business may be exchanged for property held for investment. Similarly, property held for investment may be exchanged for property held for productive use in a trade or business. For the real estate investor, the major exception covers "stock in trade" or other property held "primarily for resale." This exclusion is intended to bar "dealers" in real estate (as distinguished from investors and businessmen) from obtaining the benefits of tax-free exchanges. There are companies that now specialize in tax-free exchange arrangements. But consult with your tax advisor first.

CHAPTER 7

Renters Beware!
Legal Issues for Co-Owners— and Tenants

THE LEASE AGREEMENT

If you are considering renting your condominium unit to a tenant, you should understand a number of things before you sign the lease agreement. For example, most condominium documents require that the lease agreement conform to the particular laws of your state governing condominiums as well as other applicable statutes. Consequently, the association may require you to use a lease prepared by the association's attorney and provided to you by the association so as to ensure that it complies with the laws governing condominiums of your particular state.

A typical condominium lease agreement in Michigan will: (a) require the tenant to comply with the condominium documents and rules and regulations implemented by the board; (b) provide that a tenant's failure to comply with the condominium documents and rules and regulations constitutes a default under the lease agreement; and (c) provide that the Board of Directors has the power to terminate the lease in the event of a default by the tenant and even evict the tenant and seek money damages if the default is not cured after 15 days written notice to the co-owner of the leased unit.

THE "RENTERS"

If you have already read my chapter on restrictions, rules, and regulations, you should understand that when you buy a condominium unit, you give up certain liberties. If you rent your condominium unit to tenants, you not only give up certain liberties, you expose yourself to potentially significant liability. For example, let's say you decide to rent your condo unit to Jethro, who is a bit of a burly construction worker type, but seems like a nice enough guy. You enter into a one-year lease with Jethro. Unbeknownst to you, however, Jethro is a slob, he has a girlfriend named Daisy who likes to blast loud music, and Daisy has two screaming children! Further, Jethro has three vehicles, two rust bucket cars with blown engines and a work truck with "Jethro's Painting Company" plastered all over it.

BYLAW VIOLATIONS BEGIN

The first problem you face is the fact that you have two carports assigned to your condo unit and Jethro has three vehicles. The first week of Jethro's tenancy is relatively quiet, but for two consecutive days during the second week, Jethro arrives home from work with the inoperable rust buckets in tow. Jethro and his paint-covered buddies, who help him with odd painting jobs from time to time, literally push the rust buckets into the carport parking spaces and slide blocks in front of the tires to keep the cars from rolling out into the street. Jethro decides to park his truck in the street lengthwise behind the two rust buckets so that the truck is straddling the two carport spaces. The truck is now partially blocking one of the lanes of a major thoroughfare through the condo project.

Jethro has a big commercial painting contract, which is the reason he decided to move to Michigan and rent your condo unit. Every evening when he arrives home from work, he has at least a dozen empty paint cans in the bed of his pickup truck. There is only one trash container on the condominium premises and, pursuant to the rules and regulations, it is reserved for "household waste" only. Each night, however, Jethro tosses the empty paint cans in the trash container and by mid-week, it is overflowing. So he starts setting them on the ground around the container. The board president has a bird's eye view of the trash container and soon notices the issue, which infuriates her to no end.

Further, the association's president begins receiving several complaints from neighboring co-owners that Jethro's girlfriend Daisy has been blasting her music so loud it is causing pictures to fall off the walls inside neighboring units with shared walls and that her children have been, at times, screaming uncontrollably and throwing obnoxious temper tantrums. In fact, the shrieking of the little girl is so over-the-top that one of the co-owners actually called the police to perform a welfare check on the children. The co-owners surrounding your condo unit are infuriated that they have to deal with such disturbances from a mere renter. In fact, it is common for co-owners of a condominium project to view renters as "second-class citizens," since they do not have a vested ownership interest in the condominium project and, particularly, when they are viewed as "troublemakers."

LEGAL ACTION IS TAKEN

Next thing you know, you get a courtesy notice of violation in the mail from the association's managing agent demanding: (a) that Jethro immediately cease and desist dumping his paint cans in the trash container; (b) that the loud music and other disturbances must stop immediately, and last, but not least; (c) that the pickup truck and the rust buckets must be removed from the premises immediately or they will be towed at your expense. The violation letter notifies you (for the first time since you have not read your condominium documents) that commercial and inoperable vehicles may not be parked anywhere in the condominium project. The letter states that if you fail to correct the violations within 15 days, the matter will be turned over to the association's attorney.

SELF HELP

You speak with Jethro since you are trying to comply with the association's demands while preserving a cordial relationship with your tenant. Jethro assures you that he will get control over Daisy and the children, but he claims he came to Michigan to find work and that all of his family and friends reside in his home state of Mississippi. Consequently, he claims he has nowhere else to park the vehicles. He claims he will park the truck elsewhere and have the rust buckets running in "no time flat," so you decide to cut him some slack.

A few weeks go by and you assume the issues have been resolved. Then, you get a certified letter from the association's attorney reiterating the prior demands and advising you that you are now responsible for the attorney fees incurred by the association in connection with the matter, which now total $325. The letter further states that if the violations are not corrected immediately, the association will tow all of the vehicles, evict the tenants, and you will be responsible for the costs and attorney fees incurred in doing so. You get very upset and try to call Jethro, but he will not answer the phone. The next day, you get a call from Jethro who is madder than a hornet because there is a tow truck hooking up to his work truck. He has been advised by the driver that he will be back shortly to tow away the two rust buckets as well. You get into a heated argument with Jethro because he is now costing you more, in light of the attorney fees and towing bill you are probably going to get from the association, than he is paying you in monthly rent.

All of this aggravation could not have come at a worse time for you since you are scheduled to go on a business trip to China for a month and your plane leaves tomorrow. You try to call the association's attorney, but you are advised he is in court for the rest of the afternoon. You are so overwhelmed by the situation, you decide your interests will be best served by focusing on your business trip and dealing with the tenant situation when you return. While you are in China, however, the situation gets worse. Jethro has retrieved his pickup truck and the two rust buckets from the impound yard. He has parked them, once again, in the same places they were parked before they were towed. He continues to throw his empty paint cans in the trash container, and the neighboring co-owners have complained that Daisy and the children are more disruptive than ever. The association commences eviction proceedings against Jethro and the rest of his clan at your expense and, instead of contesting same, they move out leaving the two rust buckets behind for you to deal with, among other surprises.

LEGAL NIGHTMARE

When you return from your business trip, you have a stack of mail from the association's attorney. One of the letters advises you that you now owe the association, in addition to your monthly assessments, $2,825 in costs and legal fees incurred by the association because of Jethro's numerous defaults under the condominium documents. Another letter advises you that there has been a water leak in your condo unit and it caused damage to the unit below and the common elements. The letter further advises you that the association gained emergency access to your unit, as permitted by the bylaws, to investigate the water leak and mitigate the damages, and you will be responsible for the expenses incurred by the association in doing so. You did not receive the numerous telephone calls from the association's attorney because you did not have international calling while in China. The letter further advises you that the association will not be held responsible for any damages that may have been caused to your unit in gaining emergency access.

The next day, you decide you had better visit your condo unit to check on the status of things. You also call the association's managing agent, who has advised you that the association gained access to your unit by using a locksmith and has extracted the water, which appears to have emanated from the washing machine, which overflowed because a sock was clogging the rinse tub drain. When you enter your condo unit to check on it, you soon realize you have a mess on your hands. As you enter the condo unit, you notice that the children have been coloring the walls you freshly painted for their tenancy with crayons and markers! You also notice a strong, musty odor and, as you walk down the hallway, you notice the carpeting has turned shades of purple, green, and red from the mold that developed before the association was notified of the water leak. You turn the corner to the laundry room to realize that the washing machine has, in fact, overflowed while you were gone. What a mess!

You now have even more serious legal issues with the condominium association because of the damage caused by the water leak. Once all of the costs and attorney fees incurred by the association in connection with the myriad of issues caused by Jethro and his clan, who are now long gone, are assessed to your account as permitted by the condominium's bylaws, you owe the association more than $15,000. Further, the association is threatening to record a lien against your condo unit in order to secure its claim and file a lawsuit against you, if necessary, for money damages and foreclosure of its lien. Moreover, the association has advised you that it is entitled to recover its costs and attorney fees incurred in obtaining and collecting said judgment. You consult with an attorney, who advises you that the association is on solid legal ground and that you only stand to lose more money if you let the matter proceed to litigation. The attorney explains that you will not only have to pay her costs and attorney fees in trying to defend you, but the association's costs and attorney fees if the association prevails, which is likely. So, you use that hard-earned money you had stashed away for a "rainy day" to pay the account in full to end the madness. Meanwhile Jethro and clan ride off into the sunset in that pickup truck, presumably to ruin another unwitting landlord's life.

LESSONS LEARNED

While condominiums can be wonderful places to live for people who do not want the responsibility to maintain a single-family residential home and property, the lesson to be learned is that when you rent your condo unit, you are ultimately responsible for the actions of your tenants and their guests. Another important thing you should be aware of is that the association, at least under Michigan and Florida law, has the legal right to intercept rent payments from your tenant if you fail to pay your assessments in a timely manner, and if your tenant complies by paying rent directly to the association, it does not constitute a breach of the lease agreement.

Finally, many associations have amended their condominium documents to impose rental restrictions limiting the number of units that can be rented at any given time. So, before you purchase a condo unit as an investment property, make sure you read and understand the condominium documents. You may not be able to rent your condo unit and, even if you can, you may end up on a lengthy list of those waiting to rent their units if the limitation on rentals has been met.

The rationale behind rental restrictions is that condominium units are about shared ownership, and investors or speculators who often reside out-of-state or are even corporations are purchasing foreclosed condo units, often at "fire sale" prices and driving down the value of the units owned by the rest of the co-owners. Furthermore, it is believed by many that renters will not respect the property they rent or the rights of others, as they do not have a vested property interest in the condominium project and they typically do not know and follow the rules. As with most rental situations, the nature of the experience will often be dictated by whether you have "good" or "bad" tenants. In a condominium context, you must remember that renting to a "good" tenant can be a rather uneventful and positive experience, while renting to a "bad" tenant can be an absolute nightmare!

WHAT A TENANT SHOULD KNOW!

On the other hand, if you are considering renting a condominium unit as a tenant, there are certain things you should be aware of before you sign the lease agreement. Consider the following example.

Derek was advised by his employer that he is being transferred from the company's headquarters in Texas to its regional sales office in Michigan. The move is for at least two years, but it may be temporary, so Derek decides to rent instead of buying. He checks the classifieds and finds a perfect condominium unit in a great community close to where his new office is going to be located. He calls Randy, the co-owner of the unit, and schedules a time to view the unit. After a ten-minute walkthrough of the unit and the rest of the complex, which includes a spa and workout facility, Derek is convinced it is the right place for him, so he signs a two-year lease agreement.

Six months go by, and Derek is thriving in his new position. His sales figures are through the roof. He is also enjoying his rental unit; particularly the amenities that come along with it. The surrounding community has a great nightlife and lots of great restaurants. He is having the time of his life until, one day after work, when he goes to use the workout facility, he discovers that his key card won't work. He visits the on-site manager's office and is astounded when he is advised that the key card was deactivated because Randy has not paid his association dues. The manager says: "No dues, no gym, it's as simple as that." Derek grabs his cell phone and tries to call Randy. He leaves a message for Randy, who had previously explained to him that he travels often and may not be accessible for weeks on end. He waits a few days and is highly annoyed. He has paid his rent to Randy like clockwork for the past six months; yet he can't use the workout facility? He decides to give Randy the benefit of the doubt and realizes he really cannot do anything about it until Randy calls him back.

Two more weeks pass, and Derek still has not heard from Randy. He gets home from work one day, and there is an envelope posted to the door addressed to "Tenant/Occupant." It's a letter from the association advising him that since the association dues have not been paid, he must pay his monthly rent payments to the association instead of to his landlord. The letter further advises him that, under Michigan law (and in most other states), his compliance cannot be considered a breach of his lease agreement. Finally, the letter states that the association will commence eviction proceedings against him if he fails to pay his rent. Derek feverishly tries to call Randy to see what is going on, and Randy finally answers the phone. Randy apologizes and says that he has been in Africa for a month with his live-in girlfriend, Kelly, and forgot to make arrangements so that the association dues would be paid while he was away. Randy explains that he just got back in town and that he will "take care of" the association right away. He apologizes and tells Derek to continue to send his rent payments to him and that he could deduct $200 from his payment next month for his inconvenience. Feeling reassured, Derek mails another rent check, minus $200, to Randy the next day.

Derek then hops on a plane to Texas, as he will be spending two weeks tying up some loose ends back at company headquarters. When he returns to Michigan, he finds a mortgage foreclosure notice posted to the door of his rental unit. He tries to call Randy and gets no answer. Derek is getting very irritated with not being able to get in touch with Randy, so he decides to go work out and blow off some steam. He can't wait to try out the new running shoes he bought while he was in Texas. As he is walking down the hall, he can tell that they are the most comfortable running shoes he's ever owned. He hopes to have the running track all to himself. He reaches the door to the workout facility, swipes his card, and a red light flashes "access denied." Fuming mad after several attempts, Derek storms down the hall to talk to the on-site manager. Derek can't believe it, Randy still has not brought his account with the association current! He tries to call Randy and, again, no answer.

STUCK IN THE MIDDLE

Derek returns to his rental unit and decides to take another look at the mortgage foreclosure notice. The mortgage company has declared a default and has scheduled the unit to go to sheriff's sale in two months. Apparently, while Derek has been paying rent to Randy, Randy has not been paying the association or his mortgage company. Randy has probably been spending the money on Kelly. Derek does not know what to do about the situation, so he goes to see his attorney, Lara. He is advised that as far as the mortgage foreclosure is concerned, he will have at least eight months in the rental unit before the bank takes legal title to the unit. In addition, he is advised that there is a federal statute that provides, as long as certain requirements are met, that the mortgage company must honor the lease agreement he has with Randy so, in actuality, he has eleven months left in the unit. Derek has a problem, however. Randy owes the association thousands of dollars, and the association has the legal right to evict him if he does not pay his rent payments to the association. The attorney advises Derek he has some options. First, he can pay rent to the association for the next eight months, but once the bank takes legal title to the unit, in addition, he will have to pay monthly rent to the mortgage company in order to avail himself of the protection of the federal statute. Consequently, his rent will double after eight more months! Second, he can sit back and not pay anything to the association and hope that the association does not evict him. Third, he can bid in at the sheriff's sale and try to purchase the unit, subject to Randy's right of redemption. If he chooses this option, he must hope that the association does not try to evict him in the interim. Fourth, he can find another place to live. Derek thanks his attorney, Lara, and advises that he will need some time to think about his options.

A few days pass by, and Derek receives a notice that the association is evicting him. As much as Derek likes the rental unit, the workout facility, and the surrounding community, he decides it would be best to find another place to live. He has a problem though—he only has about one month to do it in light of the pending eviction proceedings, unless he wants to start paying the association. Derek eventually finds another place to live, but he has experienced a considerable amount of stress and aggravation as a result of getting caught up in Randy's legal troubles with the mortgage company and the association. Moreover, he has gained ten pounds since he has not been able to work out regularly!

So remember, when you rent a condominium unit, your landlord's legal problems may quickly become your legal problems. You may want to ask some inquisitive questions of a potential landlord, such as whether the assessment and mortgage payments are current to try to reassure yourself before you sign on the bottom line. You may also want to give yourself the right, but not the obligation, to make those payments, if necessary, and ask a condominium lawyer before you sign any lease.

PART II The Operation of a
Condominium Association

Now that you know best how to select, buy, and sell a condo, it's time to consider how condominium associations are supposed to operate—and how they actually do operate.

CHAPTER 8

Cast of Characters
The Board of Directors

Naturally, there are potential problems associated with the operation of the condominium association, just like any other organization. I have offered suggestions concerning the prospective purchaser's investigation of a condominium and the co-owner's need to continually monitor the affairs of the condominium association. There is an old axiom (at least, I have asserted it for more than 40 years) that a condominium association is only as good as its members, but especially its directors.

The role of a condominium board is not dissimilar from the role of the board of any other corporation. The role the board plays is the most important factor determining the success of community association operations. The board can, literally, make or break a condominium association. If the board is ineffectual, unreasonably dictatorial, myopic, vindictive, ignorant, inflexible, naive, unenlightened, penurious, self-serving, and/or unwilling or unable to adhere to the condominium documents and general corporate law, the association is in for a heap of trouble!

What is the role of the board? The board administers the affairs of the project in accordance with state law and the condominium documents. It maintains, repairs, and replaces the common elements for which the association is assigned responsibility under the condominium documents.

The role of the board includes long-range planning of the financial and physical condition of the condominium. That means establishing procedures for maintaining the condominium, collecting assessments, enforcing condominium restrictions, rules and regulations, and the like. The board also sets procedures for the holding of annual and special meetings of the association, for executing the necessary contracts on behalf of the association, and seeks to ensure that the reasonable needs and concerns of the co-owners regarding the administration of the condominium project are met.

The board of directors is the administrator of the condominium association. It establishes policies regarding the functioning of the association within the jurisdictional limits set by state law and the condominium documents.

WHAT MAKES A GOOD BOARD?

If the board is so large and unwieldy that the association's business cannot be conducted in an efficient manner, that alone may detract from the successful operation of the condominium association. For example, nine directors for a 45-unit complex is too many, even though it is commonly said that there is safety in numbers. Not so in condominiums ... except, perhaps, in the swimming pool!?

In order for a board of directors to be effective, it must intelligently carry out its responsibilities. That may require that the board employ a management firm and other consultants to help the board discharge its responsibilities. What is important to remember is that the board has the obligation, in most instances, to pick the management company, lawyer, architect or engineer, insurance agent, and other contractors or consultants that the board needs to help it discharge its responsibilities. If the board members do not understand the condominium documents and do not seek legal counsel or other consultants to help them understand and interpret the condominium documents, they cannot properly discharge their responsibilities. In fact, in too many instances, boards do not discharge all of their responsibilities.

The single greatest problem that I have observed in the operation of condominium associations over the years is the almost universal unwillingness of boards of directors to spend money. Any honest, service-related person associated with community associations will concur. For some reason, the directors believe that their primary responsibility is to SAVE MONEY, sometimes at whatever cost!

The board of directors needs to establish a feasible maintenance program for the association. Not that it must paint everyone's unit every year. However, the board must properly maintain and repair those common elements of the condominium for which the association has legal responsibility in a timely fashion. What is reasonable maintenance and repair is within the discretion of the board. If the board is extraordinarily frugal and refuses to make necessary repairs to the common areas, disenchanted co-owners may have redress against the board for the association's failure to maintain those areas, regardless of the economic condition of the association.

A board that is unwilling to spend the money necessary to properly maintain and administer the condominium is a board that is not doing its job. Admittedly, how much to spend on maintenance may be a matter of judgment on the part of each board. However, some boards have hidden behind the thinly masked veil of "discretion" in repair priorities to justify their unwillingness or inability to meet the needs of association members.

Certainly, the standard of care in an FHA-subsidized condominium project will differ from that in a project with units priced in excess of $500,000. On the other hand, I have observed condominiums with units ranging in price between $75,000 and $100,000 that were better maintained by the association than projects whose units cost in excess of $400,000. Usually, this has been the result of the board of the lesser-priced condominium having adopted a more aggressive maintenance policy than the more expensive project which has a country club mentality.

The role of the board includes assuring that the decisions of the board are uniform, consistent, and enforced vigorously with dispatch. The board should enforce prohibitions within the condominium documents concerning exterior modifications, dogs running loose on the common elements, parking in areas not designated for such, unreasonable activities by co-owners that are a disturbance to neighbors, and the like.

Unfortunately, in almost every condominium, the board, at some time or another, has made exceptions to the dictates of the restrictions, rules, and regulations of the condominium. For example, not unexpectedly, one finds that directors have friends in the condominium (at least initially) and, therefore, they are sometimes unwilling to enforce bylaw restrictions or the rules and regulations against their friends.

SEEKING OUTSIDE HELP

On multiple occasions, I have experienced painful situations where name-calling, and even physical assault, has occurred among board members and/or members of the association enraged about the operation of the association. Verbal fights over the selection of a management company (or whether to obtain professional management or a lawyer), over the selection of a snow removal contractor, or whether the developer should be sued, or whether speed bumps should be installed, are but a few examples of issues that have opened schisms within boards and/or between members of the association.

Many vendors and professionals are reluctant, or unwilling, to deal with community associations. The perception is that the community association board member may lack a clear understanding of the proper operation of the association or of sound business principles, or that his actions may be arbitrary, whimsical, capricious, or unprofessional, or that he is likely to engage in the intimidation or harassment of co-owners or other board members.

The concern is that such conduct, and the perception of vendors and professionals, may deprive community associations of competent and reasonable choices for management firms, service firms, accountants, lawyers, and other consultants. How often have you heard a service-related person complain about how difficult it is to deal with a community association board?

That is not to say that all, or even most, boards of directors fall within this mold. It just seems to those of us who have dealt with condominium associations that such personalities surface at inopportune times.

ESTABLISHING SUBCOMMITTEES

The role of the board includes the obligation to establish a committee structure, appoint officers, and solicit the help of association members to assist the board in establishing and implementing policies and directives. While the board should rely on outside persons (who have no proprietary interest in the condominium project) to assist the board with matters of law, accounting, insurance, and management, the board should recruit association members to serve on committees to help discharge the responsibilities of the board.

Boards commonly appoint, among others, an architectural control committee, a budget and finance committee, a buildings and groundskeeping committee, a bylaws committee, a social committee, a welcoming committee, and a newsletter committee. Many times, these committees are composed of people who have run unsuccessfully for the board of directors, who have served on the board in the past, or who have been solicited by the board to prepare for ascendancy to a directorship.

Unfortunately, most boards of directors fail to organize a viable committee structure. An association that lacks a viable committee structure is unlikely to enjoy broad-based co-owner participation or an effective board succession. Worse yet, apathy, perhaps the greatest enemy of the successful community association, may develop.

Condominiums are particularly susceptible to apathy because the carefree living myth has been perpetuated by developers, sales agents, and the media. Most people who buy a condominium do so to disengage themselves from the operation and maintenance of their home, not to get involved in running a nonprofit corporation such as the condominium association.

The question of combating apathy in the condo association could warrant a chapter of its own. Suffice it to say that the role of the board includes eliciting support from association members regarding the activities and programs of the board, and one of the best ways to accomplish this is through a committee structure.

One way to get co-owners to participate in the association's affairs is to persuade them that it is in their own best interest to help the association function effectively. A way to sell them on that concept is to have an annual meeting with social activities.

A condominium association that our firm represents frequently has its annual meetings at a lounge. Libations are available to the members before, during, and after the meeting. While there were instances of excess, in most instances this technique has created an atmosphere in which the co-owners feel more comfortable in attending and participating in the meeting.

Conversely, scare tactics also may elicit participation by the members. Frequently, when the association is engaged in litigation with the developer, for example, the board can convince members to list defects and deficiencies, serve on committees to solicit information necessary to assist the attorney and make the co-owners recognize that their investment in the condo is at stake. In order to solicit additional support and help, many self-managed condominiums threaten association members with the substantial additional cost that will result if a professional management company is retained, or threatening or implementing an additional assessment on the members frequently generates member attention at the annual meeting.

Many associations simply cannot get good people to run for the board or, perhaps, the "good" people are not encouraged to run for the board. There also may be a situation where the directors wish to perpetuate their power, so they overtly or covertly discourage the participation of other members.

In soliciting members of the association, the nominating committee, if there is one, should "hammer home" the fact that the quality of life in the condominium will directly reflect the quality of the board and its committee structure. This theme should be continuously promoted in newsletters, circulars, meetings of the association, and the like to crystallize to the co-owner that his participation in the association is necessary (assuming that he is not a certifiable lunatic). But just don't take any volunteer who raises his hand to be on the board. I have seen that result in disaster for the association, as the director turns out to be a "condo terrorist." Look at and research the person before you leap!

But will they then do something constructive? Since the role of director requires a substantial amount of time, energy, and expertise, and since condominium association directors usually are not compensated, this "good" volunteer many times burns out, becomes disgusted, or acquiesces to the whims of the "crazies."

Ideally, the board of directors will consist of people who are willing to dedicate their time and energies to running the business of the condominium association in a professional and business-like manner. Ideally, the board will be composed of fair-minded individuals who understand the director's role, will operate in good faith, will avoid conflicts of interest and self-dealing, and will recognize that the expenditure of association funds will be necessary for the proper administration of the project and the proper maintenance and repair of the common elements.

Unfortunately, the activities of the directors are frequently different in quality from those of a "for-profit" corporation. That is simply a problem with condominium living and operation under the present governing structure.

Volunteer board members are, by definition, uncompensated, are not trained for their positions, are many times unwilling to accept the position, are too often unable to adapt to the requirements of the position, and are simply elected to the position for the wrong reasons. Simply put, directors and officers frequently lack the psychological, economic, educational, and business acumen necessary to balance the political, economic, legal, and social realities of condominium living within the framework of the community association.

Notwithstanding the "crazies," a smart co-owner will engage in some activity to promote the successful operation of the association, if for no other reason than to monitor the affairs of the association and its board to protect his investment and peace of mind. The perceptive co-owner will investigate the infrastructure of the condominium association board and assess whether its members fit any of the personality categories set forth in this book. This monitoring process should be ongoing, particularly if there are changes in the composition of the board.

An enlightened co-owner should investigate the "cast of characters" on the board of directors, since the board will have a direct and profound impact, for better or for worse, upon the co-owner's experience with life in the condominium. Prospective purchasers also should try to gauge the directors' economic and educational backgrounds. The co-owner should arrange, if possible, to meet one or more of them personally to get a sense of what he has gotten into at the condominium. The co-owner also should consider whether he wishes to participate in its governing structure.

As frightening as it may seem, the directors of condo associations wield tremendous power, similar to their counterparts in government, albeit on a lesser scale. Typically, condo associations are vested with extraordinary power to regulate the activities of the co-owners. For this reason, the co-owner must seriously consider whether direct input to the board of directors is necessary in order to protect his investment—and perhaps his sanity.

The types of personalities one may discover on the board of directors deserve a psychological evaluation, albeit amateurish. If these descriptions of typical community association directors concern you (as they should), take note before it is too late!

Remembering that condominium associations and their directors are microcosms of society, there will be the director who is extremely aggressive and claims, or perhaps usurps, the role of leader in the condominium. This outspoken person (I will call him a "dictator") tends to seize control of the board of directors overtly or covertly. The dictator may believe that he or she is "destined" to serve on the board for years to come. This person may be well-intentioned but, at some psychological level, generally has a need to serve as a leader of the community, if for no other reason than that he has never exercised this type of responsibility in his life. Frequently, the dictator is unwilling to share his power with other directors.

While generalizations are not always valid, I have found that engineers (or their progeny) frequently assume positions of power on boards of directors, perhaps because of their training and need for precision. The archetype "engineer" director wants things done his way, and only his way, and often wants to redo everything that has transpired before him, since it was not good enough.

You are less likely to find this type of individual in the "blue collar" condominium, where members are more likely to recognize their individual limitations, than in affluent condominiums. The "professional person" may seize the opportunity to exert his supposed knowledge and expertise over people who don't wish to confront him on the board of directors because of his personality, even though they may have greater expertise.

Of course, the dictator does not have to be an engineer. He could be a male who is constantly yelled at by his wife and finds that the board of directors offers an opportunity to assert himself. The dictator could be the housewife who has raised three kids, has never ventured into the business world, and is now frustrated that she may not have lived up to her potential. Beware of an association that has this type of leader, as he or she is too often likely to emasculate all rational voices that are not as assertive or outspoken!

If the board harbors a dictator, and the dictator is able to cause the other directors to blindly follow his dictates or whims, be they altruistic or otherwise, the board is inevitably doomed to failure. On some occasions, the dictator is likely to lead the board astray or to impose his personal biases on the remainder of the members to the detriment of the association as a whole.

If this director-tyrant also controls the association newsletter, he may be able to hoodwink the association members into thinking that his path is absolutely wise and just. However, the board that is run in this fashion, by this kind of individual, may ultimately find itself sued.

On the other hand, an assertive director can also make a legitimate contribution to the board if he is consensus-oriented, rather than dictatorial. It is important to have someone on the board who can bring diverse thoughts and attitudes together to reach some sense of order in the form of a consensus.

Lack of continuity is a huge problem in condominium governance; the dictator who has been on the board for 10 years may contribute continuity and a morbid, if not necessarily historically accurate, perspective (assuming that he is willing to share it with the other directors).

You may also find on the board the personality type that I will describe as the "schoolteacher." The schoolteacher may have no other reason for serving on the board than a messianic zeal to teach, albeit extracurricularly! Unfortunately, the schoolteacher may lack business acumen and, perhaps, common sense, and also may be easily intimidated to follow the dictates of the dictator. Although the schoolteacher is reasonably intelligent, he or she is passive and does not understand why the condo association is there to begin with. Generally, she will oppose any suggestion that the board should spend money to obtain the professional assistance of lawyers or accountants, because it wasn't in her life's lesson plan.

You may also find on your board of directors the "construction worker" personality. He ran for the board of directors because his wife told him to do so. He jumped at the chance because he was looking for a way to get out of the house in the evening!

The construction worker director is generally worthless and follows the lead of others, contributing little of import except for maintenance questions. This director can be easily manipulated by the dictator, and even by the schoolteacher, to make decisions that do not serve the best interests of the association. He is also likely to volunteer for the social committee, and his most thoughtful suggestion may be to organize an association bowling league!

In affluent condominiums, a "doctor" or two will serve on the board of directors along with a CFO of a corporation. The doctor will want to run the association in his own image and has an inherent distrust of lawyers and other "lesser" professionals. He will, of course, not want to spend money. He will likely not understand why the condominium documents must be followed. Instead, consistent with his "Hippocratic Oath," he wishes to "do no harm." The CFO will share his view and fight about every penny to be spent.

In deference to Shakespeare, I cannot spare the "lawyers." (Shakespeare would, no doubt, write a trilogy about condos, co-ops, and PUDs, were he alive.) On rare occasions, the lawyer may be a much-needed voice of reason. Too often, the lawyer board member will instead be a self-proclaimed expert in condominium law and operation who has little real experience in real estate law and, usually, less in the law of condominiums. Of course, that won't stop him from giving legal advice!

Finally, let's not forget the "successful entrepreneur." Believe it or not, a businessman can be a detriment to a condominium association. Even though the businessman may have made millions, he may be unable to appreciate that the condominium association cannot be operated like his country club, where the "boys" do as they like. Often, this type of director will be the most detrimental, since his success and wealth will command respect from the other directors. He cares little for the condominium documents and discounts the advice of the association's attorney, accountant, and management firm.

A CONTRAST

In the "blue collar" condominium project, the success of the board may depend on the education of its directors. The members of the association may have little understanding of the manner in which a community association should function, so the board will soon learn that the members are easily persuaded by an assertive style. The directors of a blue-collar project are more likely to disavow the rules, or to look for shortcuts in the enforcement of the condominium documents, and they may even accept compensation for their activities when that is forbidden by the condominium documents, but many directors are more open to educating themselves on community association governance.

In condominiums whose members are mostly retirees, the

now-retired dictator will project stubbornness or senility. The bottom line, as he sees it, is to spend no money because everyone is presumed to be on a fixed income. Beware of that kind of project as an investment or a place for your parents to live! The association will be unable to meet the reasonable needs of the condominium project and will soon become dysfunctional.

This is not to say that retirement communities are impractical, or that the presence of senior citizens on the board of directors suggests that the condominium will be a bad investment or place to live. Rather, I fear the mentality of frugality that permeates the board of directors in these environs leaves little room for business sense or proper condominium operation. So get involved!

On a senior citizen-dominated board, there may be less openness to new ideas and thoughts, and less likelihood that professional management and assistance will be obtained. Although the board of directors establishes policy, it must retain persons to carry out that policy, including management agents, snow removal contractors, lawyers, accountants and insurance agents. An unwillingness to do so breeds trouble.

The quality of the director will have a direct bearing on the success of the condominium association. It is not unreasonable, therefore, for an individual to evaluate each of the directors when buying a condominium or when deciding whether to participate in the affairs of the association. You may be able to make a difference in how your association operates, if for no other reason than your involvement on the board may prevent some "crazy" from assuming control of the board to the detriment of all.

My law firm strongly recommends that clients take part in the activities of the association from their very first affiliation with the project, whether or not the association is controlled by the developer. As a whole, our clients tend to be more enlightened than many of the directors who take control of the association— and tend to make significant contributions to the association.

Remember that a well-run association can deteriorate overnight with the resignation of one or more directors or the election of one or more new directors. It should come as no major revelation that, because of the divisiveness that frequently permeates condominium boards, a change in the swing vote of one director may have a profound effect upon the decisions reached by the board of directors on crucial issues.

Abuses of board power are not uncommon in this situation. Board members have literally been thrown off the board, without authority or justification. More typically, the "good" directors simply become disgusted with the malcontent directors who impose their crazed and senseless will on the other directors, and they run for the hills.

Battles for control of the association also are relatively common. Directors disagree concerning the operation of the association, with the result that the minority "takes its case" to association members, or to the municipality. Through perseverance and the deterioration or stagnation of the condominium, even the most unenlightened co-owners may realize the board must be changed.

THE IDEAL DIRECTOR

Ideally, the board should be composed of directors who have a sense of their responsibility, who understand the condominium documents, and who understand the condominium association is a business and that it should be run as such. They should understand that in running that business, the association needs those persons and/or consultants necessary to assist the board in operating the condominium association with the benefit of as much education as possible in regard to their position as a director.

Unfortunately, most of the time, directors do not have that sense, and they may really believe that they are entrusted with the obligation to assure that the association spends as little money as possible, whatever the cost. They are intimidated by co-owners, are unwilling to make decisions, are unwilling to stand up at board meetings to express their views and, too often reach a "consensus of ignorance," as I tell my condominium law students. Frequently, this consensus of ignorance involves an issue that requires particular expertise or knowledge, generally in the engineering or legal vein. In order to save money, the directors instead combine their "life experiences." They then reach a "common sense" consensus, which often is dead wrong.

Beware of the condo board that acts this way! This will result in nothing but adverse legal and financial consequences to the condo association. If you're on such a board, remind the other directors of their fiduciary responsibility and duty to avoid conflicts of interest and self-dealing, all of which may lead to legal liability to the members.

In a nutshell, the composition of the board is crucial in evaluating the potential success of the condo association. Do your own psychological evaluation of the directors and the co-owners living in the condominium before you buy. If you're stuck in a situation with a director who is a "dictator" or "schoolteacher" type, see what you can do to build your own consensus on the board or through the association. Recognize that the operation of the association is a political affair, and that the dynamics that make a successful campaign for public office may well be applicable to condominium living, i.e. getting good people on the board. A successful director must be a sociologist, a psychologist, a lawyer, an astute businessman, an economist, a financial planner, and a consummate leader and teacher, all combined into one. If the directors collectively lack these attributes, watch out!

By the way, lunatic directors should be placed in that area of the condominium designated for off-road vehicles and the like. If you don't believe what I have preached in this chapter, attend a directors meeting or talk with a director or owner who has had to deal with a "loony" on the board of directors!

So, you want to live in a condo ... huh?

CHAPTER 9

The Man with the Plan
The Developer and Transition to Co-owner Control

The role of the developer will now be considered in the context of the developer's control of the board of directors of the condominium association during the initial stages of operation of the condominium, which may be a period of years. The developer, if he or his designees serve as board members at the same time he is developing the condominium project, must be cognizant of his responsibilities to the non-developer co-owners.

A good developer must be multi-faceted. He must deal with the trades to get the condominium buildings completed. He must be a politician when dealing with the small percentage of determined malcontents who will be unhappy no matter what he does. He must be an economist when running the affairs of the association and establishing an adequate and realistic budget so that the co-owners will find that the assessment advertised to them by the developer is both realistic and pragmatic. And he must be a sociologist, able to determine if the restrictions that are to be imposed on the association members are both enforceable and manageable.

Conceptually, the role of the developer is to develop the condominium project—that is, construct or convert the condominium units for occupancy and prepare the members of the condominium association to take control of the project and run the condominium association. If the developer has done a good job of constructing or converting the units, has adequately funded the association, has a procedure by which the board of directors can be turned over to the co-owners in a smooth and efficient fashion, has prepared an operational procedure, perhaps including a manual of operations and a book of resolutions concerning bylaw enforcement, collection, and other matters, then the developer will have fulfilled his role and will probably not get sued by the association.

Unfortunately, many developers do not build condominiums properly. They fail to comply with minimum building code requirements or workmanship standards, or they fail to convert the condominium so the project is habitable, or even cosmetically pleasing, resulting in serious problems for the association members. The developer may not properly fund the association, or may not establish or contribute to adequate reserves for the major repair and replacement of the common elements. Too often, developers fail to cause the association board of directors, while under their control, to enforce the condominium documents, thereby allowing modifications or changes that not only don't conform to the condominium documents prepared by the developer but are outside the authority of the board of directors to approve. A typical example might be the developer-controlled board that allows a co-owner (purchaser) to extend his or her deck onto the general common elements, thereby causing an expropriation of the common elements by that co-owner without the consent of all necessary co-owners.

As previously stated, the directors of the association, be they designees of the developer or non-developer co-owners, assume legal and fiduciary responsibilities to the association and its members based on the condominium documents, common law and statutory law. The developer's failure to build the condominium properly, or to cause the association board of directors, while under the developer's control, to operate in the best interest of the non-developer co-owners, will, at best, be construed as a breach of the developer's fiduciary duties. Consequently, the developer must totally understand his role as director of the association and the liability that he potentially incurs.

This inherent conflict of interest is a troublesome problem for the developer. If he is smart, he will appoint designees to the association board who are not directly related to him. That is, neither he nor any member of his family should be appointed; instead, he should appoint persons who are associated with him but who will not be attractive litigation targets, usually because they have a minimal net worth. He should attempt, if possible, to get directors' and officers' liability insurance for his designated directors while they serve on the board of directors.

The developer should assume a leadership role in this instance. The developer should not be shortsighted, thinking that his only task is to sell and market condos and then get out. Instead, the developer should establish, through properly drafted condominium documents, a vehicle that will work both now and in the future and can be adapted to the changing needs of the association and its members. The role of the developer requires that he promote the ability of the association members to take control of the association. A smart developer will establish operational procedures for dealing with common problems, such as collecting delinquent assessments, enforcing bylaw violations, writing a code of conduct for the board, and dealing with warranty complaints. The developer should not ignore the needs of the association while he is in control or, for that matter, thereafter. The developer should establish a bond of trust and cooperation with the association members, which, in the long run, will stand the developer in good stead when developing future condo projects.

The developer has the opportunity to be a good citizen, both as the developer of the project and a member of the association. If the developer is not fulfilling this direct role, purchasers should avoid his project, and he can and should be pursued *legally* by the condominium association.

Homeowners do not like starting lawsuits. They don't like to hire lawyers, and they will look for every excuse to resolve the dispute with the developer without resorting to court. It is only when they are pushed against the wall (a wall, built by the developer, which may have cracked) that condominium associations start lawsuits.

Developers sometimes get into trouble no matter what they do. But that's not normally the case. The enlightened and prudent developer can find condo development a prosperous enterprise.

PREPARING FOR THE TURNOVER

While the condominium association is under the control of the developer, the co-owners will be virtually powerless to determine the destiny of the condominium project. Although most statutes and condominium documents provide for the formation of a "steering committee" or "advisory committee" of association members, many developers ignore this obligation. If they do comply with the obligation to form an advisory committee, they may appoint people they believe will serve the developer's interest in seeing that the condominium project is completed without interference from the co-owners. Such developers are interested in selling units, not in preparing co-owners for the responsibilities of association operation.

The appointment of a token non-developer co-owner to a

developer-controlled board as mandated by many statutes that provide for the phased transition of control of the board of directors, may be a "no-win" situation for that director—and of no real benefit to the co-owners since the developer is still in control of the association.

Then, all of a sudden the co-owners get notice of the first annual meeting to take place to elect a majority of directors from the co-owner purchasers. The result, when this occurs, is that condominium co-owners are handed control of the association without any idea as to what the operation of the association requires. When the co-owners are told to take control, they understandably are concerned whether they will thereby waive any rights that they may have to pursue the developer for construction deficiencies or other claims. It is imperative, therefore, that the developer adequately prepares the co-owners to take control of the association. If the developer is unwilling to do so, the co-owners should organize themselves and, if necessary, raise sufficient funds to retain legal counsel, an accountant, and other professional advisers to assist the steering committee to prepare for the turnover meeting.

Co-owners should beware of the developer who does not care about forming a steering committee. Be cautious of a steering committee not elected from association members. I strongly recommend to condominium purchasers that they participate in the first co-owner controlled steering committee, which will serve as the precursor for future condominium association operations. You may find it prudent to have a social gathering of the co-owners at which you propose that a steering committee be organized, if the developer refuses to do so. If there are abuses by the developer respecting construction defects or inadequate financial contributions, bring these matters to the attention of both the developer and your co-owner neighbors and solicit their help to organize the steering committee with the help of legal counsel.

This task may be your introduction to the frustrations that

come from dealing with condominium co-owners. You will no doubt run across individuals who do not want to get involved for any reason and who do not understand the need to organize before taking control of the association. They have naively accepted the notion that condominium living is "carefree living" rather than "careful living." They do not appreciate that the condominium fabric is tenuous at best. They do not understand that the success of the condominium project, after the developer has left, will directly relate to the success of its board's organization and operation. More than likely, they will be unwilling to pay for an attorney for the steering committee. Many community associations flounder, particularly at their initial stages, because the members cannot or will not organize themselves.

The exception may be if they are experiencing a specific problem with the developer that they cannot resolve on their own, or if they have some other vested interest in pursuing the developer. Perhaps for less than altruistic reasons, then, the co-owners may contribute toward the proper organization of the association, while not understanding that it is in the interest of all members that the association begins on the "right foot." (The reader interested in more information on this topic may wish to consider the author's book, *Getting Started and Staying on the Right Track, 2nd Edition*, which is referenced in the References section.)

What can the enlightened purchaser/co-owner do at this point? He can try to alert association members who have already bought as to the obligations of the developer that are not being fulfilled, or to the commitment that they must make to organize the association. He must relate analogies that they can appreciate from their own business or professional experiences, which illustrate the dire consequences when an organization is not run properly.

If there is a rallying point around which all co-owners will gather, you will find that it is when the painting has not been completed, the roads are cracking, or the basements are leaking. Such deficiencies can be used by the enlightened organizer to energize the other members of the association. On the other hand, when the developer's abuses are more subtle, such as when he has not made adequate financial contributions or has not organized the steering committee, or when the developer is "sweet talking" the homeowners into believing that everything will be OK, the organizer's task will be more formidable.

YOUR FUTURE IS IN THEIR HANDS

Unlike many other societal organizations, the condominium association must be run by its director-members, as opposed to outside participants who will assist the group. While the management company can serve as a buffer or aid to the successful operation of the condominium association, it is the board of directors that ultimately has the legal responsibility to decide how the association will function. The directors are rarely professional or experienced condominium directors. Therefore, the quality of leadership and organizational skills of the persons operating the condominium after the developer leaves will, in many instances, be deficient, if for no other reason than that no one on the board has had any experience in operating a condominium association.

That is not to say that you will be unable to solicit volunteer co-owners to serve on the steering committee or the first board of directors. There are always some who are willing to participate in the operation of any organization. However, just because someone has served on another board of directors, or on a homeowners association, does not mean that he or she is a "good" condo board prospect. To the contrary. The process by which this person was appointed or elected to the previous board may have been just as inept, arbitrary or disorganized as is the process with which you are involved. There is no substitute for experience, and there is no substitute for education.

It is surprising, but true, that a person who is a skilled businessman or an educated schoolteacher may not become a good condo director. Similarly, the manager of apartment complexes or other types of commercial enterprises may prove to be a poor condo director. What will make a person a good condo director is his understanding of the role of the director, his business acumen, his knowledge of the condominium documents and procedures, and his sociological, psychological, legal, and financial awareness. There may, in fact, be persons in the condominium association who fit that bill. Hopefully, you will join forces with them to organize the condo in a proper fashion.

You will, however, run across directors who do not have the best interests of the condominium in mind, who do not have any sense of duty to the association, and/or who do not have any idea of their role. It will be through the catharsis of the condo board meeting that you will learn about these individuals and their idiosyncrasies.

THE LEARNING EXPERIENCE

There are well-intentioned people who have the intellectual and psychological abilities to be good directors and leaders but lack relevant education, experience, and/or just a "pat on the back." How can these people develop their skills?

First, anyone serving on an advisory or steering committee or on the board of directors should clearly understand the condominium documents.

Second, such persons should understand the dynamics of group decision-making. There is usually a consensus, which may not be the composite total of the opinions of each of the individual directors as earlier noted. In essence, the board decision is a compromise. It is this process of compromise that sometimes leads to improper or inappropriate decisions by members of the board or steering committee.

Third, it is beneficial to get as much literature as possible about the proper operation of the condominium and the successful operation of the association. Various area universities teach classes in the operation of condominium associations and the potential liabilities of directors and officers. Books on condominium operation published by the Community Association Institute should be reviewed by prospective purchasers and condominium directors to help them in maintaining and operating the condominium properly.

In short, there is no substitute for education and understanding of the condominium concept. The board of directors or steering committee should hire an attorney to advise it who is well-versed in condominium association operation. Suffice it to say that the steering committee chairman's son-in-law, who just happens to be an attorney, ought not to be the association's first pick. Nor should the association select the cheapest condo lawyer in town, or a management company pawn. Rather, the board or steering committee should pick an experienced and knowledgeable attorney who is recognized as an expert in condominium law and can present to the board an effective outline for association operation.

AUDITS AT THE TURNOVER

Once a newly elected board of directors is in place and the developer has turned over all books, records, contracts, site drawings/plans and association materials requested by the board, the board should review the status of the condominium project. Optimistically, the advisory/steering committee, which preceded the board, will have done some initial work, and some of the members of the advisory committee may continue to serve as directors of the association after turnover.

The board should first determine the form of management. The alternatives that are available are:

• Self management;

- An on-site manager or resident manager (sometimes called an administrator);

- A professional management company to assist it in managing the day-to-day affairs of the association;

- A management consultant to assist it in particular needs of the condominium association, such as establishing a long-range reserve for a replacement program or even dealing with the yearly budget for the association; or,

- A combination of the above.

What things, then, should the non-developer board of directors consider when it takes over control of the association? There are four "audits" that ought to be undertaken by the board of directors. These audits should be made after the association board's attorney has provided it with a checklist of items that should be considered before the developer is released of its legal responsibilities to the association. The developer and condo member association should be prepared to deal with these audits!

THE FINANCIAL AUDIT

The first type of audit to be conducted is an audit of the condominium association's financial affairs. This is necessary since the developer has previously controlled the board of directors. The board should know exactly what the fiscal condition of the association is and whether the developer:

- Has paid to the association all the assessments it was obligated to pay;

- Has not spent association money on items which should properly have been the responsibility of the developer;

• Collected the proper amount of assessments from the co-owners; and

• Contributed adequate amounts of money to establish a reserve for replacements for major repairs in the condominium and any other mandated reserves.

Unfortunately, a newly elected board may find that the association is underfunded, or has a "loan" owed to the developer, because the developer has "low-balled" the assessments; that is, he has undercharged the amount of assessments necessary to adequately maintain the condominium association and to establish a reserve for replacements. This is particularly a problem with the conversion condominium project. At a minimum, to determine the exact financial condition of the association, the board must retain an experienced condominium accountant, preferably a CPA, to conduct a preliminary audit of the financial affairs of the association as of the time of turnover.

The developer should cooperate in turning over the books and records. Unfortunately, some developers co-mingle funds with those of their own companies, and the books and records are in a state of disarray. If that is the case, the board should have even more concern about how the financial affairs of the association were conducted before turnover, and the services of a CPA experienced in condo audits will be essential. A certified audit will be an essential tool as the association attorney evaluates possible association claims against the developer for his financial mismanagement of the condo association.

THE LEGAL AUDIT

The second type of audit that the newly elected board should authorize when it takes control of the condominium association is the legal audit. The legal audit should be done by an experienced condominium attorney. He should review the condominium documents that were prepared by the developer to ensure that they are internally consistent, legally enforceable, and in compliance with the applicable condominium statute.

He also should confirm that the documents take advantage of any recent changes to the condominium statute and general corporate law that would be helpful to the association. For example, in Michigan, a statute was passed providing nonprofit association directors, officers, and volunteer committee persons protection from certain liabilities. The statutory protections can only become operative when a condominium association approves and files an amendment to its articles of incorporation. Other amendments to the condominium documents also may be necessary to take advantage of the electronic age, for example.

The legal audit should include a review of all contracts and other legal documents relating to the condominium association. The attorney for the association should review insurance contracts and determine whether the association has the type of insurance coverage that it is obligated to have under the condominium documents. For example, the attorney should ensure that the board has at least considered obtaining directors and officer's liability insurance. The legal audit should suggest a review of finances and the physical plant of the condominium project. Finally, the legal audit should recommend that the board of directors establish a book of resolutions concerning the collection of assessments, enforcement of the condominium documents, hearing procedures pertaining to fines, agreements regarding the modification of common elements, agreements concerning disabled persons, a form lease, and other matters that may be necessary to assist in the orderly operation of the association. A legal audit should be conducted periodically.

THE PHYSICAL AUDIT

The third type of audit to be performed at the time of turnover is the physical audit. The physical audit is a compilation of the defects and deficiencies in the common elements of the project for which the developer may be responsible. The developer has a legal responsibility to turn over the project in a proper and workmanlike condition, and if warranties have been extended expressly, implicitly, or by operation of law, in a manner consistent with its terms.

The board of directors should pursue these potential claims against the developer and also should establish a budget that includes adequate reserves for future repair and replacement of the physical plant of the project. It may be necessary for the board of directors to retain architects and/or engineers to help them to do so. Finally, the board should consider mailing a questionnaire, prepared under the auspices of the association attorney, requesting that the co-owners provide information concerning defects or deficiencies in the common areas that they have observed, along with unfulfilled promises made by the developer or his representatives. The physical audit may be an ongoing process if there is ongoing construction by the developer.

The association board must consult with legal counsel, based on the results of the audit, to determine what recourse, if any, the association has to correct the defects and deficiencies in the physical plant of the condominium. The physical audit can also serve another important purpose: to evaluate the long-range useful life of the amenities of the project in order to properly fund reserves. A long-term reserve analysis may also eventually be necessary.

THE OPERATIONAL AUDIT

Finally, the board of directors should, with the advice and aid of counsel, engage in an operational audit of the project. The operational audit determines whether, in fact, the association is running smoothly and what part of its operation can be enhanced. What type of management form is best suited for the condominium association? Are there effective procedures for co-owner complaints, vehicle registration for parking, the compilation of voter designation forms, listings of the association members' names and addresses, and the like? Are board and association meetings properly and efficiently conducted? Are they to be open or closed sessions?

In short, the operational audit is an attempt to ensure that adequate operating procedures are in place and that there are procedures to streamline and clarify those processes. The assistance of a professional management company or consultant is often helpful in ensuring proper operation of the condominium association.

So, too, are operational rules and resolutions for collections, bylaw enforcement, lease forms, a code of conduct for the board, modified agreements, and formal service contracts. (See reference No. 5 on page 261.)

CHAPTER 10

Choosing Hired Help
The Condo Association Attorney,
Managing Agent, CPA, and
Insurance Agent

Among the most important considerations for the board of directors or officers of a condominium association is the need for advice and services of outside professionals to assist them in running the business of the condominium. While this may seem obvious to the lay reader, it is not a fact of life in the operation of all condominium associations.

Many times, the directors or officers of the association are individuals who have had no exposure to or need for an attorney, except perhaps in a divorce proceeding or in the defense of a drunk driving charge. On the other side of the spectrum is the corporate executive who has relied upon legal counsel his entire professional life and, since he's been successful in his business or occupation, is now "too smart" to need an attorney. These attitudes often permeate boards of directors, resulting in a general reluctance to even interview an attorney.

Also, there is the belief among some that attorneys are "expensive" or will cause additional problems rather than resolve them. While such generalizations are certainly not accurate, they occur with sufficient frequency that they cloud the thinking of many association directors and officers.

The fact is that the condominium association needs an attorney as much, and perhaps more, than in any other business. Moreover, the co-owners need legal representation to protect their interests even before they take control of the association.

The need for legal representation begins when the developer establishes, or the co-owners organize, an advisory committee. The attorney chosen by the advisory committee should advise the members of the organizational skills that will be required to prepare the co-owners to assume control of the association. If there are problems with the construction or conversion of the condominium, the attorney for the advisory committee can assist advisory committee members in getting these problems resolved. If there are financial issues that perplex the co-owners, these can also be discussed by the advisory committee's attorney with the developer and his counsel.

How to pay the advisory committee's attorney is often a source of conflict and acrimony in the initial stages of condominium development. Generally the developer, as the controlling director of the condominium association, will not wish to fund the retention of counsel by his customers. The developer may fear that if co-owners "organize," they may disrupt the development and sale of the condominium units. He may fear that getting them legal representation may result in litigation being brought against him. The developer may be simply insensitive to the need of the association to have independent representation. In any event, in most instances in which I have had experience, the developer will not appropriate funds out of the association's budget for the retention of legal counsel for the co-owners or chip in his own money.

What, then, has to ensue is that an organizational person must organize the co-owners and seek sufficient contributions from them to retain counsel. This should only be done after the advisory committee, or representatives of the co-owners, requests that the developer advance the funds from the condominium association.

A developer should be willing to appropriate association funds to retain counsel, since his attorney, who has represented him in the development of the condominium and may also be representing the association controlled by the first board of directors, cannot and should not get into a potential conflict of interest situation by representing the co-owners.

The attorney chosen by the advisory committee should prepare the co-owners to take control. One of his major tasks will be to explain to the co-owners what the turnover of the association really means. Often, the co-owners are concerned that if they accept control of the association, the developer will be relieved of his legal responsibilities incident to the commitments he has made in the condominium documents and purchase agreements. That is generally not the case, since the change in control of the condominium association is merely a change in the composition of the directors, with the result that the co-owners, for the first time, are empowered to run the affairs of the association, collect money, hire counsel, and do other things that are necessary to operate the business of the condominium project.

If the association does not retain counsel on behalf of the co-owners before turnover, it should be one of the first things the newly elected board undertakes. As previously discussed, the board should conduct a physical audit, a legal audit, a financial audit, and an operational audit, under the general direction of the association's attorney, to insure that the condominium is in a proper state of affairs.

PICKING THE RIGHT ATTORNEY

How can the board of directors be sure that it picks the right attorney? And what factors should the board consider when doing so? These questions cannot be answered without a clear understanding of the association attorney's post-turnover role, and can perhaps best be answered by citing examples of mistakes that, too frequently, the board of directors has made in doing so.

It should be clear to the reader that the attorney, particularly in the initial stages of condominium association operation, may be the board's most important consultant, because the attorney will assist the association to evaluate and address both the legal and financial problems that it is likely to find. It's hard sometimes to convince recent purchasers that they need a lawyer, particularly before turnover. Nevertheless, the association's attorney should be given the responsibility to collect overdue assessments, enforce restrictions, communicate with the developer to resolve problems with the construction or conversion and with the condominium documents, and assist the board to understand and discharge its fiduciary and legal responsibilities.

Many times, the developer has selected a management company that the new board wishes to continue using. Frequently, and logically, the directors ask the management company to recommend an attorney to represent the association.

Although management companies presumably are in a position to assess attorneys, one must remember that management companies are not immune from conflicts of interest that may influence their recommendations as to attorneys and other contractors. Allow me to use fictitious characters to illustrate some finer points.

Seymour Schlemiel has a favored attorney he recommends to the boards of directors of projects he represents. Seymour likes C.C. Cheap, since C.C. Cheap and Seymour have worked together on a number of projects and C.C. Cheap is "cheap." Seymour likes C.C. Cheap because he contributes to Seymour's strategy to find the cheapest people possible for the association, which enables Seymour to keep assessments low and makes Seymour a "hero" to the members. Moreover, C.C. Cheap does personal work for Seymour, and they share investments and an office building owned by Seymour. In a word, they are very "thick." Consequently, Seymour has recommended C.C. Cheap to at least 150 condominium associations. As a result, it has become dangerous and financially risky for either C.C. Cheap or Seymour to criticize or "blow the whistle" on one another. Of course, none of these facts are disclosed to the condominium association by either Seymour or C.C. Cheap.

Seymour recommends C.C. Cheap to the board of directors of "Blue Collar Condo." C.C. Cheap has apparent credibility since, being cheap and so often recommended by Seymour, C.C. Cheap represents many condo associations. Seymour knows that C.C. Cheap is likely to appeal to the Blue Collar board because C.C. is "low-key" and has hired a young associate from the Louisiana bayou (cheaply, of course) who, with his Southern drawl and "boy next door" demeanor, will appeal to a Blue Collar board that is uptight about lawyers in the first place.

Of course, the directors of Blue Collar don't understand that, the costs of business being what they are, C.C. Cheap is not as cheap as he represents. His hourly rates may be deceptively low; that is, he may charge 1/4 hour of his time for each phone call, regardless of length. His services may reflect his lack of competence and inattention to client needs, and he charges the same hourly rate for his new inexperienced associate. As they say, "You get what you pay for."

Since the board of directors is serving without compensation and, presumably, without appreciation from the members, it should realize (although it frequently does not) that it should hire the best attorney available to help it run the affairs of the association. The best attorney available may not be the cheapest or, for that matter, the most expensive. The best attorney available is the one who has the relevant experience and whose reputation in the legal community as a condominium expert will enhance his ability to get results from judges and adversaries. He should have the office staff and technical equipment necessary to represent the association efficiently and a reputation for fair, honest, and reasonably aggressive representation of condominium associations. Finally, the best attorney will maintain his independence from financial dependence or personal relationships with other people or entities serving the condominium project, thereby avoiding even the appearance of a conflict of interest.

In most jurisdictions, the association will have a choice of attorneys with at least 10 to 40 years of experience in condominium law. Again, the board should not fall into the trap of hiring the cheapest lawyer, or of blindly hiring a lawyer the management firm recommends, including the one it may refer to as "its attorney," or of hiring a board member's friend.

The association should review the attorney's credentials thoroughly, ask for references, and ask the proper questions of the attorney in order to evaluate his or her availability, independence, and abilities. What law school did the attorney attend? How many people does he have on his support staff? How many associations does he represent and is he able to represent all of these associations adequately? How does he calculate his hourly rate? What is the minimum charge for a phone call or a consultation? Does he bill in increments of a quarter hour, a tenth of an hour, or by some other method? Does he have any flat rate fees for collection or bylaw enforcement procedures? What is his record of success in construction defect cases, assuming this is one of the association's concerns? Is he recognized in the community as a condominium law expert? Do developers and lawyers fear him as a seasoned and competent proponent of the association's concerns, or is he a laid-back guy who will not stand up for the rights of the association? Will he stand independent of the management firm and raise concerns about abuses or problems that he may see from a management standpoint? Does he attend or conduct seminars, teach classes, write columns, articles, and otherwise keep abreast of the evolving changes in community association law? Is he available when you need him, by phone or otherwise, and can you get along with him? Is he or she free of any proprietary interest in the association or project?

After considering these factors, the board may well determine that C.C. Cheap is not their man. The board should, of course, interview him, and it should dig into his background. The board should keep in mind that what may appear to some directors to be a relatively mundane legal procedure may, as a matter of proper legal practice, be more complex.

For instance, managing agents and directors frequently question the cost to place and record a lien on a unit for unpaid assessments and, subsequently, to start collection procedures. Unless the attorney has a great deal of experience with the prosecution of collection matters, he will not know the intricacies and subtleties of federal and state debtor protection laws, or the alternatives available under the condominium documents and statutes. Moreover, the association attorney's collection expertise may be critical in determining whether the association is able to recoup its attorney fees and costs.

Generally, the attorney will charge an hourly rate based on his experience, expertise, and market conditions. An association that hires a lawyer based on cost alone will not necessarily find the right one to best pursue its interests. The association actually may end up paying more if it hires a lawyer who is incompetent, inefficient, or unable to serve his clients effectively in the relevant legal practice areas. Moreover, once the association is "locked in," the cheap lawyer may raise his rates or charge the same rate for all lawyers in his firm who possess less experience or expertise!

I do not mean to suggest that Seymour Schlemiel, our property manager, cannot be of assistance to the board of directors in its search for the best attorney. In fact, for every Seymour, there is a Joe Juggernaut, who, as a relatively independent property manager, will advise the board that it should hire the best attorney it can find, considering that many of the costs incurred by the association can be recouped from the defaulting co-owner, and that competent legal advice may enable the association to avoid the far greater expense of litigation. Will the association be able to retain the attorney on a monthly retainer basis for fixed services, or should it be on an "as needed" basis only? Finally, Joe will recommend that he examine the fee agreement between the attorney and the association.

In summary, the association should be less mindful of the hourly rate and more concerned about the caliber and value of representation that it will receive. There is no reason to accept less than excellent representation for the association, to compromise the interests of the co-owners, or to needlessly subject the co-owners and directors to potential liability. Remember the old Cantonese expression: "He who charges least knows best what he is worth." Nor should there be any improper relationship between the management company and attorney; both should be independent and serve as a "check and balance" for condominium administration. A good question to ask your attorney is whether he would be in a position to sue your management company if necessary. If he says no, you should seek another, more independent, attorney!

SELECTING THE RIGHT MANAGING AGENT OR TYPE OF MANAGEMENT

Over the many years I have been involved in community association law, I've had an opportunity to work with many types of management companies, resident managers, and administrators who have been employed by the condominium association to assist in the association's operation. Selecting the right managing agent or type of management is critical to the successful operation of the condominium association. Remember, the managing agent at the least will be handling the association's money.

First, it is important to define the term "professional management company." By that term, I mean a company that is in the business of servicing community associations with professionals who have reached a certain designation in their particular fields of endeavor, namely, professional community association managers. While some states require that professional management companies be licensed, thereby requiring a certain aptitude and/or testing, other states do not have any precondition before one can hold itself out as a professional management company. However, there are designations in the professional management field and, in particular, residential professional management, which can be obtained through various organizations, including the Community Associations Institute, The Institute of Real Property Management, and other similar organizations. While these designations do not guarantee that the person who has them is an excellent property manager, it does at least provide an insight into the willingness on the part of that person or company to obtain additional training and/or appropriate professional designations in the residential professional management field.

A professional management company can provide myriad services to a prospective community association. These services include full service, i.e. providing onsite management, handling accounting and administrative matters, and dealing with bylaw enforcement, litigation assistance, and contract bidding, all of which are indispensable in order for a successful condominium association to thrive. Other management companies may offer limited services such as accounting only, consultation regarding various matters on an hourly basis, or simply a one-time consultation arrangement in order to get its books and records in order or to prepare or review a budget.

It should be emphasized that all management companies are not alike. Unfortunately, over the years, some management companies in certain locations have tended to low-ball one another in the bidding process in order to obtain the account from a condominium association. Many condominium association board members are overly frugal and they will frequently look for the cheapest management company to facilitate its operation. Unfortunately, that has resulted in management companies not receiving an adequate return on their investment, overloading the management associates with too many associations to represent, and/or branching out into ancillary services—which, while sometimes beneficial, can also result in potential conflicts of interest and an elimination of successful competitive bidding from other outside service providers.

Obviously, professional management in the residential setting has advanced with the technological age, and many management companies now have not only computer and electronic billing and accounting but also other ancillary services that keep up with the electronic revolution. However, that does not necessarily mean that the management company with the fine-tuned computer system will provide excellent accounting or, for that matter, adequate accounting, since in the last analysis, successful management depends on the individuals and personalities involved in a management company.

What is important, however, is that an association contemplating the retention of a professional management company should learn as much about that company as possible, including getting a list of associations the management company is not only presently managing, but has managed in the past, thereby finding out what problems, if any, occurred. It is also imperative that representatives of the association visit the offices of the management company to learn exactly how the company is set up, how it functions, and what type of personnel it has manning the company functions. For example, is the management company operating out of the basement of a home or atop a beauty salon? Or is it operating in its own freestanding office space with adequate personnel and advanced technological equipment available to it?

Another important thing to remember in retaining any business, including a professional management company, is that the company is only as good as the lowest person on the totem pole. Many times the president or principal sales representative will appear at your community association board meeting presenting a very neat, clean, and exhaustive presentation about how the management company can help you. Moreover, that person may point out his or her long involvement in professional management and their particularized expertise with respect to condominium, cooperative, and/or homeowner association operations. However, it is also important to remember that while the head of the company may be "great," the person they have hired to do the accounting may be new on the block and may not have the foggiest idea as to what to do when push comes to shove. Ensure in the management contract that the person you meet is designated as your property manager. Also make it known that their leaving may be a basis for termination of the management contract.

Also, most importantly, make sure that the management contract is not signed before an *independent* attorney representing your association reviews the management contract. The management contract is the most important contract that your community association will likely sign, and many times the management company may recommend an attorney to you to review your management contract claiming that that attorney "has reviewed the management contract of the management company in many other situations and has approved it." Beware of that type of representation, since the attorney may be financially and/or legally beholden to the management company. You are best advised to find an attorney to represent you who is not held hostage financially or otherwise by the management company for providing him with recommendations and/or referrals.

For example, if the management company tells you that you do not need a lawyer to review the management contract, beware! The management contract typically has a number of provisions which could be detrimental to the interests of the association, and may leave the association financially liable without the benefit of insurance coverage, depending on the types of provisions that the management company contract proposes. Most likely, provisions regarding indemnification and termination as well as automatic renewal provisions are likely to raise questions as to the propriety of the management contract, and you should ask your attorney to review it carefully *before* you sign it.

Picking the right management company should not mean that you pick the management company that offers the cheapest per unit price or gives you a deal that you cannot refuse. Picking the right management company means that you have done your homework, reviewed, if possible, the financial status of the management company, (e.g., I have seen certain management companies that have had tax liens filed against them), gotten references from other clients of the professional management company, and ensured that you have an out clause to allow you to terminate the management contract without cause upon reasonable notice. Be sure you don't hire the abrasive, arrogant, "know it all" egotistical tyrant as your agent, either, as he or she will create controversy and legal liability for your association. Remember, the agent works for you and takes directions from you and not vice versa.

All of the above assumes that you are willing or able to go with a professional management company. Some associations, because of their physical composition, may choose to hire a resident manager. That, of course, has its own set of problems, since the resident manager may also be an owner who will then have some political stake in retaining his or her position and will have the right to assert that political standing among the members of the association. It is always best to have someone who does not have any pecuniary or proprietary interest in the condominium project to service the association, particularly in the event a dispute arises resulting in termination and potential litigation. That also applies to landscapers, lawyers, insurance consultants, accountants, and anyone else who is performing services for the association.

When picking the form of management, I do not mean to suggest that cost is not a factor. Some management companies may be totally out of line in terms of what they charge, either way too high or, for that matter, way too low. Beware of the management company that presents a per-unit cost that is too good to be true, because more than likely it is. On the other hand, there are certain management companies that charge a premium and they are well worth their cost, but again it should depend on the services that are being provided, when those services will be provided, and what their experience has been in dealing with community management matters. Of course, as in any other profession, it is extremely important to note that the more experience the professional management company has, the better your association is likely to operate.

Another important question to ask of a prospective management company is what has been the turnover of associates in the company. Frequently there is a great deal of turnover because the management company does not pay their associates enough salary and/or benefits to which they may be entitled compared with other types of property management. Unfortunately, it has been my experience that residential property management in the condominium area is the lowest paying of any of the residential property management fields, and that is sometimes reflected in the type of services that are being provided. Therefore, tight control over the management company's activities, as well as how they handle your money, is extremely important!

Unfortunately, as in any other type of business, there are occasionally defalcations (misappropriations) of funds and/or embezzlement that take place on the part of management companies and/or property managers. It is important that your books and records are maintained accurately and that you engage in the proper and frequent audits necessary to ensure the financial viability of the association and to otherwise protect it from fraud. Also, beware of the so-called "friendly" contract the management company is offering you in terms of hiring contractors, insurance consultants, and/or lawyers. Do not become involved in a tying agreement where you are obligated to utilize the professional management company in order to take advantage of purported financially beneficial insurance contracts and other types of contracts. Also, be sure to ask the association's attorney how he or she is prepared to handle a dispute with the management company should one arise. If that attorney is unable to say, categorically, "Yes I can and will do so," I would be concerned about hiring that attorney to do any work for the association, given the fact that it is important for the attorney to be in a position to advise the board of problems about the management company irrespective of whether or not his or her financial livelihood is conditioned upon that relationship.

Some management companies obviously have favored attorneys that they continuously recommend over and over again. While that is not necessarily a bad thing, it is something to be looked into in order to find out whether, in fact, there is some sort of "unholy alliance" between the management company and the attorney. Also, it is important to find out whether the persons who will be handling or servicing your account have had experience in handling community associations or they are merely glorified administrative assistants who used to do clerical work but have now been pushed up into a position of property manager because of the need to fill a vacancy or because of increased volume. It is imperative that the person you work with not only has the experience and training, but the personality and candor to deal with the board of directors. Picking a managing agent who will say "yes" to everything the board directs without question is not the best pick for your association. On the other hand, I have seen examples of a management agent who is abrasive, aggressive, and fills the vacuum of authority that a board of directors allows him or her to fill because they are either apathetic, naïve, intimidated, or unwilling to assume leadership roles. That type of management personality can undermine the association, abuse the co-owners and lead the association into potential liability and frequent litigation.

Oftentimes, larger condominium associations have the financial ability to engage their own administrator to assist the association in the operation of the condominium project. That means that they hire a full-time administrator, with perhaps another accounting person, either full or part-time, and onsite personnel to assist in landscaping, snow removal, and/or other maintenance activities. This is frequently done in large communities where a professional management company will not be able to devote the time and energy necessary to personally assist the association, or where the association recognizes that it has the financial wherewithal to have an employee working directly for the association, as opposed to anyone else, and has direct control and supervision over that person(s). That has proven to be extremely successful in associations of 250 or more units. Again, it depends on the economics of the condominium association in terms of whether that type of governance is best for the association. In any event, proper contractual documentation should be reviewed by counsel for the association before engaging any employees and/or independent contractors on behalf of the association who are performing supervisory or management responsibilities.

If you are interested in retaining a truly "professional" management company, get various referrals from independent sources before you interview them. Interview at least three different companies and set up criteria in advance, which must be satisfied before a decision will be reached on a hire. It is always a good idea to have your attorney present at that interview process, as your attorney may have had experience in dealing with the management company in the past or, for that matter, will know the right questions to ask to ensure against obfuscation and double-talk, and to otherwise determine which firm will be able to work with the management company to deal with the typical problems of collecting assessments, bylaw enforcement, and other governance issues.

Management assistance is essential to the successful operation of the condominium association. Determining the right management assistance, while sometimes time-consuming and arduous, is well worth the effort—even if after thorough investigation, the condo association decides to become self-managed by its board of directors.

PICKING THE RIGHT CPA AND INSURANCE AGENT

Generally, when the association picks a CPA or insurance agent, the managing agent or attorney may be a source of referral, but the board of directors should conduct an independent evaluation of the candidates. The association should avoid hiring a professional who in any way is involved with or related to the association, either as the owner of a condominium or an immediate relative of an owner. Indeed, this applies to any professional considered by the association. A CPA should be hired to audit the association's books and to assist the board to set up a financial structure at the condominium. If the association has a professional management company, the latter should work with the association's CPA to satisfy the tax laws and place the record keeping aspects of association operations on a basis consistent with sound accounting and business principles.

The insurance agent that the association hires should not be picked because he is a cousin of a board member or is our friend Seymour Schlemiel's sister-in-law. Rather, the insurance consultant should be able to provide an objective and valuable service to the board in ascertaining the nature, extent, and amount of insurance necessary to safeguard the association and its directors and officers. He or she must have a keen knowledge of the insurance problems unique to condominiums, such as the scope of coverage to the units and common elements, indemnification protection for the association and the directors, and more. The board of directors will use the advice of these service-related persons to make important decisions that are the board's responsibility. They should not be picked arbitrarily or capriciously. Each consultant should maintain a perspective of independence and, ideally, should be the "cream of the crop" in their profession.

Of course, when things go wrong, the persons who scream the loudest about the assessments going up will be the first to jump on the board if it makes a mistake in judgment because it did not pick the best consultants or other professionals. That's human nature and is as much the case in condominiums as anywhere else. There is no reason, therefore, for a board to shortchange itself when hiring attorneys, property managers, CPAs, insurance consultants, and other professionals necessary to help the board discharge its affairs. The "penny wise, pound foolish" maxim applies, and it should be avoided at all costs.

CHAPTER **11** Skeletons in the Closet
Potential Problems for
Condominium Associations

The intent here is to alert the reader to some of the relatively unique problems of condominium association operation that might not be considered by the novice board member.

Being a director is a thankless job that calls for the application of keen managerial skills to a unique business operation. Typically, the person who accepts a position on the board expects that it will require only that he or she attend a few evening meetings and make a few decisions concerning the amount of assessments, the person who will be the landscape contractor, and the like.

Unfortunately, condominium operation, as with most other types of business operation, is becoming increasingly complex.

For example, 30 years ago no one talked about radon gas and its potential ramifications. However, the significance of the prob-

lem of radon gas for condominiums is potentially awesome—
they are ingredients that are indigenous to certain types of
structures or land that may prove to be potentially hazardous to
the health and safety of humans. (The reader may desire to substitute "asbestos," "mold," "uri-formaldehyde," "arsenic," or
"soil contaminants" for radon gas.)

Is the condominium association equipped to deal with such
problems? Has the association inherited a condominium project
that was converted from an apartment that contained dangerous
levels of uri-formaldehyde? Does the condominium sit on property that contains excessive levels of lead or mercury or an under-
ground oil or gasoline storage tank? What are the consequences
for the association if this is the case? Does the association have
any responsibility to ensure that these are not a menace? What
about potential civil liability to the association under state and
federal environmental laws?

Problems with the environment may be expected to remain a
major source of concern in condominiums. Garbage disposal,
sanitary sewer problems, water supply, flooding, and, in some
instances, air pollution, also will be among these. The very fact
that condominiums may be deemed "quasi-municipalities" by
the courts will focus additional attention on the "due process"
and "equal protection of the law" rights that condominium
co-owners have vis-à-vis the association.

It was not shocking that some courts have deemed the operation of a condominium to be analogous to "state action," with
the result that the members of the association are afforded con-
stitutionally guaranteed rights vis-à-vis the association and its
directors, and this is likely to increase.

And then there is the area of employer liability. Yes, the association may hire employees, particularly if the board of directors
has opted for self-management. What happens when the manager is accused by the assistant manager, who is an Asian female
with a disability, of making unwanted remarks that are sexually

suggestive, or that disparage her gender, ethnicity, or physical ability? Does the board of directors have a sense of its responsibility and the potential liability to the association under federal and state civil rights statutes and other applicable laws? Discrimination can exist in a condominium hierarchy and management structure, as in any other commercial setting. Claims of the violation of one's "civil rights" in employment and living opportunities are becoming increasingly prevalent in condominiums. The board of directors normally has no appreciation of the extent of the association's potential liability or the attendant attorney fees and costs that may result if litigation is commenced. Condominium associations are not immune, moreover, from civil rights intervention by the Justice Department on behalf of condominium residents. The Federal Fair Housing Act strictly prohibits discrimination in residential housing against the "handicapped" and, with the single exception of qualified senior housing projects, discrimination based on "familial status," among other earmarked classifications.

The association's board, as well as its managing agent and legal counsel, should have a keen understanding of the civil rights and employment laws. Many states have undermined the concept that a person can be terminated from his or her employment without cause. Board members erroneously tend to disregard employment concepts, both because they are serving as volunteers and because the nonprofit corporation is not designed to make money. On the other hand, while the directors of a condominium association may be exposed to liability to the same extent as a director of a "for-profit" corporation, they may not have the same concern for insurance protection.

Another area that may pose problems for condominiums is the air space and water rights of condos and their environs. Disputes have arisen concerning the rights of upstream or downstream users in streams and navigable waters that pass through a condominium and the rights of the condominium association to maintain exclusive use of portions located within the condominium boundaries. In one instance, an association was concerned because the restrictions were not specific on whether a seaplane could be docked at the condominium boat wells, which were on a lake.

Finally, one should not underestimate the security responsibilities of condominium associations. Increasingly, co-owners expect the association to maintain adequate security within the confines of the condominium premises. Guardhouses may not be enough. Additional lighting may not be enough. The budgets of associations may have to be increased to provide a heightened level of security, not only because the association members wish or expect it, but also because the courts and the events of 9/11 and Hurricane Katrina may mandate it.

In short, the sky and the crust of the earth are literally the limits when considering changes that may take place in condominium operations and the need, therefore, to revise restrictions, rules and regulations to anticipate them. Forward-thinking drafters of condominium documents must consider the potential changes in technology and the environment and their potential impact on the condominium project. Surely these are questions that should be revisited by attorneys, developers, associations, management companies, and legislators.

CHAPTER **12** Crime and Punishment
Condo Rules are *Not* Made
to be Broken

Perhaps one of the most important things a prospective purchaser of a condominium unit should understand is that common ownership does not necessarily mean common interests. I recently read an apt quote attached to an e-mail from one of my clients, which stated: "We could learn a lot from crayons: some are sharp, some are pretty, some are dull, some have weird names, and all are different colors ... but they all have to learn to live in the same box." The same holds true with co-owners in a condominium: some are smart, some are not so smart, some are attractive, some are not so attractive, some have hard-to-pronounce names, and they may have a wide array of varying nationalities and backgrounds ... but they all have to live in the same condominium project.

RULES AND RESTRICTIONS

Constant bickering can run amok with all the varying personalities, backgrounds, and beliefs in a condominium project. Just like the laws that govern our daily lives, however, there are laws, restrictions, rules, and regulations governing ownership of a condominium unit; otherwise there would probably be chaos and condominiums would be unmanageable—and sometimes they are. The laws, restrictions, rules, and regulations are designed to provide certain rights and responsibilities and otherwise provide for harmony in communal living and the maintenance of optimum property values. Even in light of the laws, restrictions, rules and regulations, however, there are still significant disagreements over their application and interpretation.

When you own a condominium unit, you must understand that you are required by law to abide by the applicable rules and restrictions in the condominium documents. Furthermore, your tenants and/or guests are required to abide by the applicable rules and restrictions in the condominium documents, and you may be ultimately held responsible for their actions or omissions. You should read and understand the condominium documents before you buy! While you are reading the condominium documents, you should also keep in mind that the condominium documents, and some of your rights and responsibilities thereunder, could usually be amended upon a 2/3 vote of the co-owners and their mortgagees. What does that mean? It means that what is allowed now may be disallowed five years from now, and vice versa. Certain things existing before the vote may be "grandfathered" in, but the point is that you give up certain liberties when you buy into a condominium project.

HOME BUSINESSES / RIGHT TO LEASE

The condominium documents may restrict or prohibit a whole host of activities. For example, the documents may restrict the use of your unit to residential use only. So do not be surprised if your dreams of opening a day care facility in your new condo unit are crushed by the board of directors. The documents may also limit the number of units you may own. The documents may further restrict or prohibit your right to lease your unit and govern the terms of any lease agreement. The documents will likely further govern whether you may make alterations to the exterior appearance of the unit or any structural modifications to the unit unless you live in a "site" condo.

ACTIVITIES

The documents will also likely dictate whether you may display a "for sale" or "for rent" sign in your front window or yard, whether or not you may install a Jacuzzi or hot tub, whether or not you may have a basketball net in your driveway, whether or not you may have certain furniture or other personal property on your porch or balcony, and/or whether or not you may conduct a garage sale. I know this is America, but some condominiums actually prohibit you from barbecuing at all, citing safety concerns, and those restrictions are generally enforceable. The documents will typically prohibit reptiles, exotic pets, or other animals, but most documents provide an exception for a certain number of dogs and/or cats. And yes folks, it is hard for me to say—being a dog lover and all—but there are some condominium associations that actually prohibit co-owners from maintaining any dogs or cats whatsoever! I personally have two dogs who reside with me in my condominium unit—Bailley and her younger companion Joyleih. Bailley the "Legal Beagle" and Joyleih the "Assistant Legal Beagle" also work at our law firm, typically on Fridays, and they both provide valuable insight to the office staff and attorneys regarding, among other things, legal issues affecting dogs, as well as enhanced mental health for the personnel. So if you are thinking about buying a condo, read the documents to make sure your faithful companions Fido the dog and Socks the cat are allowed.

PETS

So you have checked the documents governing the condominium unit you are thinking about purchasing and the association permits co-owners to maintain two dogs or two cats, or one of each. Did you also notice that the documents require the dogs to be on a leash at all times and that they may only be walked and/or exercised in certain designated areas? If you think you are simply going to open the sliding glass door to your unit and throw out a tennis ball for Fido to fetch, guess again. Furthermore, did you notice the provision in the documents that requires dog owners to immediately collect and dispose of their dog's fecal matter? If you are taking Fido for a walk at the condominium project, you had better take some plastic bags with you! In addition, did you notice the provision in the documents that prohibits dogs whose barking can be heard on a continuous basis? If Fido suffers from separation anxiety and barks incessantly while you are at work, do not be surprised if the association sues you seeking a court order requiring removal of Fido from the premises!

Some documents provide height and weight restrictions regarding dogs. Our law firm believes those types of restrictions are arbitrary, capricious, and unenforceable, and there are court rulings wherein judges have struck down those provisions on that basis. Although Bailley and Joyleih do not run the risk of exceeding height and weight restrictions, they are firmly against them. In fact, they highlighted the absurdity of the provisions by pointing out the fact that great Danes, which far exceed the typical restrictions in terms of both height and weight, are fondly referred to as "gentle giants," whereas pit bulls, which normally fit within the typical height and weight restrictions, are known for their sometimes vicious and violent behavior. Of course, a dog's behavior is usually a product of their upbringing, but the point is that you need to read the documents; otherwise, you may find yourself in an expensive and protracted lawsuit fighting to keep your beloved canine companion.

THE CATCH-ALL

The condominium documents typically will also contain a catch-all provision generally prohibiting a co-owner from engaging in any activity, which may be immoral, improper, unlawful, or offensive. The catch-all provision will also typically prohibit the co-owner from engaging in any unreasonably noisy activity in their unit or upon the common elements. Finally, the catch-all provision will usually prevent a co-owner from engaging in any activity that will raise the association's rate of insurance, or from engaging in any activity that may be a nuisance and/or annoyance to the other co-owners.

CHILDREN

I generally counsel clients against purchasing an attached condominium unit if they plan to raise a family. Think about it; children, by their very nature, are oftentimes unreasonably noisy. And if you think your neighbors are going to think that boisterous Zach and little Samantha are the wondrous bundles of joy that you and your spouse believe they are, you are most likely wrong! You may soon find that your child's frequent temper tantrums will trigger complaints from your neighbors, which could quite possibly result in fines being levied against you by the board of directors and/or a bylaw infraction letter from the association's attorney threatening to sue you and, if state law and the condominium documents allow, assessing the association's costs and attorney fees incurred in seeking your compliance with the condominium documents against your account.

COOKING

What if you love to cook with curry, which is notorious for triggering complaints in condominium projects? Curry is a mixture of spices that emit a strong odor, and there have been instances where neighbors in a condominium will complain that the smell from curry has traveled into their unit or the common areas causing eye, sinus, and throat irritation. You may think you have the right to cook whatever you please in your own home; after all, it is your condominium unit, right? Your right to cook whatever you please, however, may be curtailed when exercising that right results in a nuisance or annoyance to your neighbors, rendering you in violation of the catch-all provision prohibiting it.

MOTORCYCLES

If you think your new neighbor at your new condominium unit is going to think your new Harley-Davidson with the loudest Screaming Eagle exhaust pipes on the market (and your tattoos) is the best thing since sliced bread, you are most likely WRONG! In fact, I will bet that he will despise you and your new motorcycle, particularly when you come rumbling into the condominium project at 3 a.m., waking him up from a dead sleep. This is particularly so when he has to leave for work at 6 a.m. I would further bet that he will be cursing your mere existence as he tosses and turns for the remaining few hours of precious time he has left to sleep before he must get up for work.

I would further bet that your new neighbor, who is crabby as hell at work that day, is going to complain to the board of directors and/or the managing agent about his sleepless nights. The board of directors will then have an obligation to investigate the matter, as the board has a fiduciary obligation to enforce the condominium documents. A few days later, you get a notice in the mail, probably from the association's managing agent, advising you that operation of motorcycles on the condominium premises is absolutely prohibited. The notice further demands that you cease and desist operating your motorcycle on the condominium premises. You are astonished and dismayed at the prospect of not being able to ride your brand-new Harley. The notice further advises you that in the event you do not immediately cease and desist, the matter will be referred to the association's attorney, at which time the costs and legal fees incurred by the association will be assessed to your account. You then think to yourself: "They can't stop me from riding my new Harley, and they certainly can't dictate what may be stored in my garage! After all, it is not like I am storing enriched plutonium in my garage!" So, you continue to ride your Harley in defiance of the board of directors and, in particular, your new neighbor. A week goes by without incident, except for a few disapproving looks from your neighbor.

A few days later you get a letter from the association's attorney (someone like me who will sound like he has a real axe to grind) advising you that Article VI, Section 7 of the Bylaws states that the "use of motorized vehicles anywhere on the condominium premises, other than passenger cars, authorized maintenance vehicles and commercial vehicles as provided in this section 7, is absolutely prohibited." The notice further states that the association will allow you to continue to keep your motorcycle in your garage, but that you must walk the motorcycle from your garage out to the main entrance of the condominium project and vice versa. As you look down at your prosthetic leg and over at your 600-pound Harley-Davidson, you think to yourself, "They will not get away with this!" Truth is, however, should you choose to hire an attorney and fight enforcement of the bylaw provision on the basis that it is unreasonable, you will probably have an expensive lawsuit on your hands, and you had better make sure you have the financial and mental wherewithal to endure the legal battle. At the end of the day, you may well lose the legal battle and not only have to pay your attorney's fees, but the attorney fees incurred by the association as well!

RETIREMENT

Some people say condominiums are the perfect place for retired folks to reside, but that may not be true for the retired widow whose hobby happens to be gardening. Again, read the condominium documents before you buy and keep in mind that the provisions may be subject to change. So, 75-year-old Ellie decides to purchase a condominium unit because she is a widow who can no longer take care of the maintenance associated with owning a single-family residential home. She does not bother to read the condominium documents and decides one day that spring has sprung, so she starts to plant vegetables outside her new condominium unit. She will soon find out much to her dismay, however, that the association has a rule that states: "Fruits, vegetables, climbing vines and climbing flowers will not be approved and are not permitted." Sorry about your luck, Ellie, you should have read the documents and the accompanying rules!

And what about 70-year-old Olivia, who is the proud new owner of a condominium unit? One of Olivia's hobbies is woodworking. In fact, Olivia is very excited about spending most of her retirement building cabinets in her wood shop in her new garage. Olivia too bought her condominium unit without first reading the condominium documents. Olivia's excitement soon turns to deep disappointment when she finds out that the documents require her garage door to be closed at all times, except for ingress and egress. In other words, she may open the door to leave, but must close it right behind her and vice versa. Olivia thinks to herself that the natural light and fresh air of an open garage are integral parts of her woodworking hobby. In fact, she will likely become overwhelmed by sawdust if she keeps her garage door closed. She planned on spending many hours each day in her wood shop. Olivia has a big problem, and there are further issues she faces beyond keeping the garage door being closed while she is enjoying her hobby.

Woodworking creates a lot of dust and noise from the power saws and sanders. Remember that pesky little catch-all nuisance and annoyance provision I mentioned earlier? Soon, her neighbors will inevitably start complaining to the board of directors regarding the dust and the noise, and Olivia's retirement dream will be destroyed. If only she had read the documents, Olivia would have realized that condo living is not for her.

KNOW AND FOLLOW THE RULES

The bottom line is that, legally, you give up certain liberties when you buy a condominium unit, and you had better make sure you are willing to follow certain rules and regulations before you buy, because your dog Ruffles may not be allowed. Violating the condominium documents may result in serious consequences. The documents often provide that delinquent co-owners may not vote, sign petitions regarding association matters, and they may even be prohibited from serving as a board member or officer of the association. Perhaps the most serious consequences are a lawsuit being filed against you, a lien being recorded against your condominium unit, and, among other things, a judgment for money damages and foreclosure being entered against you. At the end of the day, if there is equity in your condominium unit, keep in mind that Ellie and Olivia paid cash for their units, the association may take the unit to sheriff sale and you may be evicted from your home. Yes folks, you could lose your home if you fail and/or refuse to follow the rules and regulations. Condominium ownership is serious business indeed, so read and understand your documents with the help of an experienced condominium-wise attorney! On the other hand, those rules, regulations, and restrictions are designed to make the condominium development a better, safer, more desirable, and aesthetically pleasing place to live.

CHAPTER 13

'Show Me the Money!'

Assessment Collection: The Lifeblood of the Association

I suspect that at least some (perhaps most) people who have never owned a condominium believe that when buying a unit and thereby becoming members of an association of co-owners, they must only contribute nominal sums of money to pay for snow removal, lawn maintenance, and possibly plant a few flowers out by the entrance sign. Once you purchase a condominium unit, however, you soon realize that becoming a member of the association might require much more in terms of a financial contribution in order for the association to operate efficiently and properly.

As mentioned earlier, a condominium association is typically a nonprofit corporation that relies on the collection of assessments to provide services and management to its members. The association is comprised of members, i.e., the owners of the condominium units, and the association operates through its duly authorized board of directors. Board members never cease to amaze me, as they serve as volunteers and it can truly be a thankless job at times. Ever hear the saying, "No good deed shall go unpunished"? I would not be a bit surprised if it were a condo board member who coined the phrase. While board members are motivated by a plethora of things, typically the position is sought so that the member will have a say in the day-to-day operation of the condo association, thereby protecting the particular board member's investment. Board members have a vested interest in the association's affairs, and the decisions they make usually have a direct impact on property values. If a board member feels any sense of accomplishment from serving the association, however, it can oftentimes be a beleaguered sense of accomplishment.

Money is the lifeblood of the association, and big debt cannot be tolerated. I always advise clients to have an aggressive assessment collection policy. Co-owners are delinquent in payment of their assessments and are filing for bankruptcy protection and/or facing mortgage foreclosure at an alarming rate these days. It is vital to the survival of the condominium association that delinquencies be vigorously pursued and collected. The board has a fiduciary responsibility to ensure that the assessments are collected in a timely manner and that the association's budgetary needs are adequately funded to fulfill the maintenance, administrative, and operational obligations of the association.

Some co-owners probably think their obligation to pay assessments is a joke, but let me tell you from 40 years of experience, it is no laughing matter. Typical assessments for the garden variety association I represent run anywhere from $200 to $500 per month. Tack on the costs, interest, late charges, and attorney fees that are charged to the delinquent accounts, and it adds up quickly. The longer the delinquency persists, the more the charges escalate. Consider the following extreme, but possible, example:

THE COLLEGE STUDENT AND THE "SNOWBIRDS"

Maisy is a 23-year-old college student who resides in her parent's condominium unit in Michigan. Her parents, Joan and John, have gone to Florida for the winter. Her parents have essentially "left her" the condominium unit and in exchange she has agreed to "take care of" all of the bills associated with it—although her parents have not deeded her the unit and, consequently, still own it. A couple of months go by and, aside from paying the utility bills, Maisy has not paid assessments levied against the condominium unit because she just had to have that new Gucci purse from Macy's instead.

THE LIEN

Maisy comes home from school one day and finds a letter from the association stating that the assessments are delinquent and that interest and late charges have been assessed to her parents' account. The letter further states that the matter will be turned over to the association's attorney to record a lien against the unit if John and Joan fail to contact the association to make payment arrangements to bring their account current. Maisy sets the letter on the kitchen counter with the rest of her "junk" mail because she is more concerned about having adequate funds for that Lady Gaga concert she and her girlfriends are attending this weekend. She tells herself that she will pay the association eventually. She thinks to herself: "It's just the stupid condo association, they can't do anything to me!" So she goes to the concert and spends the money she should have spent paying the assessments, and it will be two more weeks until she gets paid from her job waiting tables at TGI Friday's.

THE FINAL LETTER

A few more weeks go by, and the association turns the matter over to its attorney. The association's attorney sends a letter to John and Joan stating that a lawsuit for foreclosure and money damages will be filed against them if they do not contact the attorney's office to make payment arrangements. Remember John and Joan? They are soaking up the sun in Florida and playing Mahjong with their fellow snowbirds, completely ignorant of what is going on with their condo unit in Michigan! The final letter, however, is delivered to the condo unit, because John and Joan never advised the association or the post office of their forwarding address. John and Joan are relying on Maisy to sort through and forward their mail. Maisy reads the letter, but realizes that if she tells her parents about it now, she will be in hot water, and they will likely come back to Michigan immediately because she cannot be trusted to handle their affairs. Maisy is enjoying her newfound freedom, and she has a ski trip planned with her girlfriends to Aspen over mid-winter break, and she does not want to take a chance on ruining her trip! Maisy is not going to make any payments to the association at this time because she has to save every penny she has made over the past couple of weeks so she will be able to enjoy her ski trip. After all, she does not want to have to drink Five O'clock Vodka while her girlfriends are enjoying Grey Goose!

THE LAWSUIT

While Maisy is enjoying the ski slopes and her Grey Goose whilst soaking in the hot tub in Aspen, the association's attorney files a lawsuit against John and Joan for foreclosure of the association's lien and for money damages. A process server's attempts to serve John and Joan are unsuccessful, however, as no one answers the door. The process server prepares an affidavit after several attempts, indicating that the unit appears to be occupied and that there is a vehicle in the driveway, so it is the process server's opinion that John and Joan are simply evading service. The association's attorney then obtains verification from the post office, which confirms that the condominium unit is, in fact, John and Joan's last known address. The association's attorney then prepares a motion asking the court for an order allowing for alternate service of the summons and complaint. The court issues an order allowing the association to post a copy of the summons and complaint on the front door of the condominium unit and to mail it to the unit address. The association's attorney complies with the order for alternate service and files a proof of service with the court. Now, John and Joan have 28 days to answer the complaint—and they are still in Florida for another three months!

Maisy comes home from her ski trip Sunday afternoon and sees something posted to the front door. She does not have time to be bothered with it though, as she has all sorts of things to unpack, not to mention the five loads of laundry she has to do before she returns to work—and her school classes resume on Monday. A month goes by and, although she brought the envelopes from the law firm in the house and set them on the counter with the rest of her "junk" mail, Maisy has not opened them ... she figures it is just the association reminding her that she owes delinquent assessments. Maisy does not realize, however, that it is not only the assessments that are continuing to accrue, there is a $50 late fee tacked onto the account each month it is delinquent, along with legal costs and attorney fees and 7 percent interest on the unpaid balance, which has now gone from several hundred to several thousand dollars.

THE JUDGMENT

A month goes by, and the next thing Maisy gets is a notice from Bob at the law firm that a default has been entered by the court against John and Joan in the lawsuit. Maisy does not open it though, and it goes in the pile with the rest of the unopened "junk" mail. After all, Maisy is busy studying for exams and she just started seeing a new boyfriend. Yet another month goes by, and John and Joan arrive home just in time to learn that a default judgment has been entered against them giving the association the right to foreclose on the condominium unit or seek to collect on the money judgment that has been entered against them in the amount of $14,756.28! Further, the association has the right to collect costs and attorney fees incurred in collecting the unpaid judgment. John and Joan have lived in the condominium for so long their mortgage is paid off, but they keep to themselves and this is the first year they went to Florida for the winter. John and Joan quickly realize the association could take their unit to sheriff's sale and evict them if they do not pay off the judgment! John and Joan decide it is time to contact the association's attorney and make payment arrangements. Maisy is going to have to get a second job if she is ever going to repay her parents, assuming they do not disown her!

While the above example is extreme, inasmuch as the parents really got duped, I had a case one time where two college-age sisters bought a condominium unit and became delinquent in assessment payments. The young ladies never responded to the letters from our law firm, and the association eventually obtained a judgment for foreclosure and money damages against them. Once we started collecting on the judgment, however, the sisters went to their father, who contacted our office and bailed them out by paying off the judgment. By that time, the judgment was almost $9,000!

Most co-owners are responsible, and even though they may fall on hard times and become delinquent in payment of their assessments, they eventually contact our office and make payment arrangements. The problem is, the longer you wait the more you will owe! If you want to put *my* grandchildren through college, that's perfectly fine by me, but don't say I didn't warn you!

JUDGMENT COLLECTION

We have found that there are unique and creative ways to collect judgments. All you have to do is use your legal imagination. There have been cases where the delinquent co-owner owns his or her own business and our office has been successful in obtaining money judgments in favor of our clients directly against those businesses as a consequence of garnishment proceedings. In one case, the association had a judgment against a co-owner who owned a bar, so we commenced garnishment proceedings against the bar. When the bar failed to respond to the writ of garnishment, the court entered a default judgment against the bar. Our office then obtained an order from the court to seize property, and we sent the sheriff to the bar to seize all of the cash in the cash register. The co-owner passed away several months later, and he did not have sufficient funds to pay all of his debts. While under normal circumstances our client may have had to write off the debt, our client still has a judgment against the bar. Our office served an order to seize property on the State of Michigan Liquor Control Commission and thereby seized the liquor license. Our client was then in a position to sell the liquor license to satisfy the judgment.

In another case, the delinquent co-owner owned a beauty salon, and our client obtained a money judgment directly against the beauty salon as a consequence of garnishment proceedings. We sent a court officer to the beauty salon to seize money from the cash register, and we requested that the court officer pay particular attention to any bank statements, checks, withdrawal slips, and/or deposit slips in an attempt to find out where the salon banks. It turned out that the co-owner who owned the beauty salon was working that day. As the court officer was sifting through the cash register, he found a deposit slip. Bingo! The beauty salon banked at a credit union right around the corner. The sheriff looked at the co-owner. The co-owner looked at him. It was off to the races.

The co-owner ran out of the salon, got in her car, and drove straight to the credit union. The court officer, however, was not far behind. When the court officer entered the credit union, the teller was about to hand the co-owner a couple thousand dollars in cash. The court officer handed the teller the order to seize property, flashed his badge, and advised the court officer he would seek to hold the teller in contempt of court if she proceeded to turn the cash over to the co-owner. Needless to say, our client ultimately recovered the cash from the credit union.

PAY YOUR DUES

If you are thinking about purchasing a condominium unit, you should realize that you may be paying not only for snow removal, lawn care, and the occasional planting of flowers, but also for maintenance, repair, and replacement of certain common elements of the condominium project like the roofs, walls, and roads. In addition to contracting with vendors who provide various services to the association such as lawn care, snow removal, roof replacement, etc., most associations hire a management company, an accountant, and a law firm as well. And remember, if you don't pay your assessments, the burden falls on your neighbors to pick up the tab. While some delinquent co-owners ultimately also lose their unit to mortgage foreclosure, remember: The association can still get a money judgment against you for which you are personally responsible. So unless you file for bankruptcy protection and obtain a discharge of the debt, you may end up finding that your wages, bank accounts, and/or personal property are being seized by the association pursuant to a court order in order to satisfy the judgment. Our law firm even has several cases where the association is pursuing collection of judgments against former co-owners who have moved outside the State of Michigan. You can run, but you cannot hide! The bottom line is that if you have the money to pay your assessments, pay them! Even if you cannot pay the assessments in full, you should contact the association and make arrangements to repay them over time. Do not bury your head in the sand and hope that the problem will go away—because it won't. Delinquent association accounts are like a snowball rolling down a hill. The longer the snowball rolls, the larger it gets! Simply put: Pay now or pay a lot more later. Also, the sooner the association commences collection procedures, the better chance of collecting!

CHAPTER 14

Empty Promises
When the Developer Walks Away from the Project

As we all know, the economic downturn of the late 2000s caused economic strife in the real estate industry and, in particular, the development and operation of community associations throughout the country. As a consequence, developers have literally walked away from projects, turning them over to the lender, going bankrupt, and/or just leaving them half complete without any concern about the further operation of the condominium association—while still maintaining control of the association or letting it dissolve.

This has resulted in myriad potential legal entanglements for the co-owners and the condominium association depending on the circumstances of each case. In many instances, scavenger investors have come in to buy the lots for ten or twenty cents on the dollar and, in some instances, developers have repurchased their lots from the lender who foreclosed on their development at an earlier time for pennies on the dollar. In other situations, no one has reclaimed the lots and they have been sold at county tax sales—with investors from around the country blindly purchasing lots in the condominium and, in some instances, finding themselves to be deemed a "successor developer" under the Michigan Condominium Act with consequential liability.

What is consistent in all of these situations is the hardship that is imposed on the co-owners, who often do not know what to do or what is happening. In some of these developments, so-called "site condos," the co-owners do not even realize that they bought into a condominium project, as it looks like a normal subdivision. They do not find out that they actually own a condominium in a condominium subdivision until they try to sell or otherwise refinance their properties—or in the case of the prospective purchaser, until they seek financing from a lending institution. The federal government and real estate companies are of no help because they are allowing these units to be sold at rock-bottom prices in an effort to liquidate at whatever cost.

What can the members of these associations do to help themselves? They will, of course, first call their congressman, their state legislator, their mayor, the building inspector, and perhaps their local religious leader in an effort to see whether help can come from anywhere other than their pocketbooks. They may well flounder around for years until they find an external leader besides the Almighty who has the intestinal fortitude to recognize that they need expert and immediate legal assistance to put the pressure on those parties who will ultimately pick up the pieces at the condominium, either as developer or other entrepreneur at the project.

Too often, many years go by before the homeowners recognize that they have rights that can be asserted, but only through experienced legal counsel that knows which buttons to push in order to get results. Generally, successor developers have liabilities under state statutes. Those who are in that position may still have a responsibility to the association to pay assessments, etc. Moreover, the developer and/or successor developer and the former directors of the association may be personally liable for their acts or omissions.

Often we have found that developers who have abandoned one particular project may well be willing to take care of certain items in the project because they have obligations to the municipality—and have put up bond money or other types of guarantees, and they are concerned about their reputation in other developments in this community or other communities.

The size of the developer may also be important. National developers who usually hide behind a limited liability company for a particular project often advertise their national company name or trademark in sales literature and purchase documents, which causes them to incur potential liability as joint venture developers. We have been successful in many instances in holding national developers responsible for the acts of their limited liability company in a particular project with limited or no assets because of the manner in which they have handled their advertising. So-called "quality builders," for example, have used the parent name on all their literature and websites.

There is, of course, no shortcut or easy answer to the economic problems caused by a defunct developer. Indeed, some associations are going into the developer business themselves by way of completing the project and selling off units to prospective purchasers on land that was previously earmarked by the developer for construction. Also, the association may end up owning or controlling common element portions of the land that were earmarked for development, if after a certain number of years, the developer abandons the development or fails to otherwise complete units in the project.

In short, there are a number of situations where condominium associations can emerge from the financial abyss with a relatively strong financial position, and the co-owners will not have vacant and abandoned property surrounding their condominium units. One word, though, about condominium boards and their efforts to resolve issues with scavengers who come into the condominium project. My experience is that directors of community associations, particularly those who have reached a certain degree of personal business success, often think that they are much more capable of resolving their issues gentlemanly (or ladylike as the case may be) with developers as opposed to using legal counsel effectively. It defies imagination that directors would think that developers, investment companies, and other entrepreneurs will somehow feel more generous in dealing with board members directly than through their legal counsel. To the contrary, when a board says to the developer, "We think we are spending too much money on legal fees and want to deal with you directly," it is a sure sign to the developer that it has prevailed and is in a position of strength. Certainly, the developer would prefer to negotiate with a layperson board than experienced legal counsel—no matter how sophisticated the board may be. No matter what, the developer thinks he has a psychological advantage in that situation.

This is another example of a board being naïve—and penny wise and pound foolish—because any experienced negotiator will recognize that when the board says they are running out of money and/or do not want to use their lawyer, that is the best time for the other side to pounce on them and extract a more than advantageous resolution. Trying to keep boards in line in any kind of litigation against the developer, a successor developer, or any other difficult party is one of the most challenging aspects of representing community associations. Trying to get directors to use common sense in dealing with the negotiation process is too often very taxing and frustrating. Often, the board will ask the attorney to do things that he or she thinks is totally wrong, and the question becomes whether the attorney has a responsibility to pursue the directive of the client or say, "I have had enough and you ought to get another lawyer since you are not listening to me." I have often asked boards that when their doctor tells them to do something, do they go to their insurance consultant to get a second opinion because a couple of the board members took health in grade school? Do they know better than the doctor as to what type of treatment should be undertaken? The same holds true for legal advice. And if the board has confidence in their attorney, they should follow his or her advice.

In any event, the problems attendant with abandoned projects are not going away. The best advice I can give to anyone in that situation is to get a good lawyer who has the experience of dealing with the parties who now have a vested interest in completing the project in some fashion for the developer who has skipped town.

CHAPTER **15** Frisky Business
Condoms, Condominiums, and
Conception

Inexplicably, I recently found myself pondering the question of whether there is any nexus between the words "condom" and "condominium," other than sharing a prefix. While it may be that I was simply bored while waiting for a flight at the airport, I think I may have stumbled across the answer. There may be no greater place on earth that couples should wear condoms than while having sex in their condominium units! Bear with me folks; I know what I am talking about.

THE NOISY NEIGHBOR

As previously noted, condominium documents typically contain a catch-all provision generally prohibiting a co-owner from engaging in any activity that may be immoral, improper, unlawful, or offensive. The catch-all provision will also typically prohibit the co-owner from engaging in any unreasonably noisy activity in their unit or upon the common elements. Finally, the catch-all provision will usually prevent a co-owner from engaging in any activity that shall raise the association's rate of insurance, or from engaging in any activity that may be a nuisance and/or annoyance to the other co-owners.

Conceptually speaking, of course, it is fairly difficult to have sex without making noise, and some people are noisier than others. Furthermore, depending on the integrity of the furniture you are relying on to support the activity, there can be squeaks, bangs, rattles, and the occasional almighty crash or gasp. The combination of noises from the people engaging in the act and the furniture supporting it has the potential to be disturbing to neighboring co-owners, particularly if your 7-year-old son wakes you up in the middle of the night and asks you why someone, who is breathing really heavy, is pounding on the shared wall next to his bed. I don't know if the use of condoms could lessen the noise, but it's a theory worth testing out.

THE HOT TUB PARTY

While there are many instances where sex can cause problems at a condominium project, let's talk about the infamous all-night hot tub party for a moment.

Ed is a 30-year-old marketing executive. He is single, popular with the ladies, and has money, to boot. Ed lived with his parents while he attended college and missed out on many social activities because he wanted to focus on his studies and graduate at the top of his class. After working for a couple of years and scrupulously saving his money, Ed bought his first condominium unit, and it's right next to *yours!* There are four units per building, and while you carefully selected an end unit to ensure the most possible privacy, you now share a common wall with Ed. You meet Ed for the first time and think to yourself: "There shouldn't be any

problems, Ed seems like a fine young lad . . ." Then, the unspeak-
able happens—an installation crew shows up Monday morning
to install Ed's new hot tub! You're out of town on a business trip
for a couple of days, but by the time you get home Thursday
night, the installation is complete. You walk into your bedroom
to unpack your suitcases, and you notice a curious humming
sound. So you decide to investigate.

You look outside, and there is a hot tub right near your bedroom window! You decide to try to live with it, but the pump
motor cycling on and off all night long is slowly driving you
crazy. Then comes Saturday night, and things really start to escalate! You see a leggy blonde getting out of a car in Ed's driveway
just before dusk. Things are quiet for a while and then another
couple arrives at Ed's place. You think to yourself: "They must
be having a dinner date," as you put on some relaxing music,
grab a glass of wine, and sit down on the couch to read a novel
you have been dying to start ever since it made the bestseller list.

You are really enjoying the novel. It's been a couple of hours
and it feels so good to relax after your hectic and stressful trip.
Besides, you have completely shut the humming noise out of
your mind, at least for the time being. Then you hear Ed's door-
wall slide open, and he and his guests are now outside drinking,
laughing, and partying in his new hot tub. You look at the clock
and it's 11:05 p.m. It's getting late and you're about ready to go
to bed—you want to get up early and do some shopping before
you have to return to work on Monday. You retire and hope for
the best, but the hooting and hollering seems to be getting worse,
as the revelers are clearly getting inebriated, as they were not
obviously drinking Faygo pop. It's now 2 a.m. Although you had
hoped the partying neighbors would be passed out by now, no
such luck. It's loud, it's obnoxious (you can hear Ed's girlfriend,
Joanie, laughing it up), and you just can't take it anymore. They
are making water balloons out of condoms and throwing them at
each other. You are about ready to open your window and yell

obscenities, but you are not the confrontational type, so you decide to call the management company.

You get a voicemail greeting, of course, as it is clearly after business hours. The recording says to call the police in the event of an emergency. You don't want to call the police because you do not want to deal with it any longer that night, so you stuff your ears with cotton and bury your head in the pillows hoping to shut out the noise. But remember that shared wall we talked about earlier? It just so happens that your bedroom and Ed's bedroom have a shared wall and the leggy blonde, Joanie, is in rare form tonight! The next day, there are condoms all over the lawn.

After numerous complaints, both verbally and in writing, to the association's managing agent about the hot tub, the association fails and/or refuses to correct the problem. So you make an appointment to see an attorney. You are advised that not only is the hot tub a nuisance and an annoyance, in his opinion, but the attorney believes Ed had no right to install the hot tub on common elements. In fact, Ed has unlawfully expropriated common elements. The attorney writes a letter to the management company on your behalf and demands that the association insist Ed remove the hot tub at his expense forthwith, or he will recommend that a lawsuit be filed against Ed and the association. After months of letter writing and settlement negotiations, Ed finally agrees to remove the hot tub and reimburse you for some of your attorney fees, but it costs you thousands of dollars in attorney fees to get to the end result.

There are certain things condominium associations can control by putting certain restrictions in the bylaws, but in many instances, co-owners such as Ed fail to read and/or understand the bylaws, and it takes an actual bylaw enforcement action—and, many times, involvement of attorneys—for the violations to be corrected either voluntarily by the co-owner or as a result of a court order. While condominium associations generally have the right to recover costs and attorney fees incurred in obtaining compliance with the condominium documents, co-owners typically do not have that right unless the condominium documents so provide. Living in a condo can be wonderfully enjoyable when everyone follows the rules, but it can be an absolute nightmare if they don't!

CHILDREN AND CONDOS

Finally, let's talk about conception for a moment. I have always been of the opinion that apartment-style condominiums and multi-unit high-rise condominium buildings are not an appropriate place to raise children. Let the record reflect that I do not have anything against children. In fact, I raised two of my own and love them and my grandchildren dearly. But if you think you are going to buy little Randy that Red Ryder BB Gun for his birthday (which is a rite of passage for many American boys growing up) and you're not asking for trouble, guess again!

Generally speaking, most condominium documents, at least for most of the condominium associations my law firm represents, have bylaws that contain, among other restrictions, the following provision: "Activities which are deemed offensive and are expressly prohibited include, but are not limited to, the following: any activity involving the use of firearms, air rifles, pellet guns, BB guns, bows and arrows, illegal fireworks, or other similar dangerous weapons, projectiles, or devices."

Consequently, while little Randy may own and possess the BB gun in his condominium unit, he will not be able to shoot the BB gun on any of the common elements and his natural desire to do so may be more than little Randy can bear!

And that would be a clear violation of the condominium documents and a slam-dunk bylaw infraction matter for which the co-owners of the unit (i.e., little Randy's parents) will be responsible, including all of the association's costs and attorney fees incurred in correcting the violation.

While most young boys dream of having their own BB gun,

they have no right to fire them on the condominium premises where people are living in close proximity.

Another example of where conception can cause trouble in a condominium is when you own an upper-level unit and you are thinking about buying little Randy that basketball he's been begging for. Don't do it! What's the first thing he is going to want to do with the basketball? Bounce it!

You have hardwood floors and the neighbor below you, Dr. Goss, has already complained to the association's managing agent about the pitter patter of little Randy's feet running up and down the hall! How do you think your neighbor is going to feel about a basketball?

You may say to yourself: "I will tell Randy he can only play with the ball outside. That will avoid any potential issues with Dr. Goss in the unit below." Do you really think Randy can resist bouncing the ball inside? Moreover, do you even know whether the association allows children to play basketball on the premises? You say to yourself: "I will make Randy play with the basketball at his schoolyard, which is within walking distance of the condo." Do you really think Randy can make it out of the condominium project without bouncing his basketball on the way out?

Most people are sensitive to noise, albeit some more than others. And there will be complaints. Furthermore, that basketball could end up costing you hundreds and possibly thousands of dollars if the problem persists and the association decides to pursue you in court seeking an injunction—a court order requiring Randy's parents to stop little Randy from bouncing the basketball at the condominium project.

The bottom line is that while condominium projects with attached units are typically great places for retired folks, couples with no children, and young single professionals, they are generally not desirable places to have and raise children. Detached condominiums or site condos, however, are more conducive to raising children. So my advice to you is if you are going to buy into a condo project with attached units, make sure you are "doing it" as quietly as possible—and make sure you wear a condom!

Seal of Approval
Why Most Condominium Projects Want FHA Certification

Starting with the real estate and banking meltdown in 2005, the country's real estate market was in a state of collapse, mortgagees were rapidly foreclosing, banks were closing daily, and few financial institutions were lending money for new home purchases. Real estate was no longer attainable for most Americans. The American dream was in jeopardy.

MAJOR CHANGES TO FHA (1934 - 2009)

In 2008, President George W. Bush passed the Federal Housing & Economic Recovery Act (12 USC 1708(a)(5)). Following that Act, the Federal Housing Administration (FHA) stepped up to insure condominium unit mortgages so that lending institutions would bear less risk because the FHA would pay a claim to the lender in the event of a default in the repayment of the loan by the mortgagor/co-owner. To protect itself, the lending institutions, and the real estate investors, the FHA passed new regulations on Nov. 6, 2009, abolishing "spot" approval (i.e. individual condominium unit approval) and requiring project-wide certification for an entire condominium project before it would insure condominium unit loans. (FHA is an insurer of private lender mortgages, not a lender itself.)

Thus, no longer could a purchaser of a condominium unit obtain a mortgage insured by the FHA unless the entire condominium project was "certified" by the FHA, with the exception of so-called "site condo" projects.

The FHA was established in 1934 to increase home construction and reduce unemployment at a time when the country was primarily a nation of renters (only one out of four homes were owned by its residents). FHA now insures a major portion of the real estate mortgage market (more than 40 percent as of 2011). FHA insures forward and reverse mortgages, up to 30 years, in FHA-approved condominium projects.

GET FHA CERTIFIED TO ENHANCE MARKETABILITY

Obtaining FHA certification can greatly enhance the marketability of the condominium units for resale and for refinancing. Not having an FHA-certified condominium project often results in lending institutions refusing to give loans and offers to purchase units falling through because the buyer cannot secure financing. As we navigate through the difficult economy, it is necessary to eliminate unnecessary obstacles and create every advantage possible. FHA certification for eligible condominiums is one assured way in which unit resale marketability can be improved. (To determine if your condominium project is currently FHA certified, you can review the condominium list online at: https://entp.hud.gov/idapp/html/condlook.cfm.)

The 2009 FHA requirements mandate criteria for obtaining,

recertifying, and maintaining condominium project certification. Condominium projects deemed eligible for certification are projects that are: 1) primarily residential (i.e. at least 75 percent residential), 2) are in full compliance with state and local condominium and other applicable laws and regulations, and 3) meet all of the certification/recertification criteria established by the 2009 FHA requirements, as amended (which happens regularly).

Condominium projects that do not require project-wide certification are most site condominiums (i.e., the "unit" is the land/air space) and commercial condominiums (i.e., over 25 percent of the overall project), among a few other types. Other condominium projects ineligible for project-wide certification are where the developer has retained ownership of amenities, time-share condominiums, condo hotels, multi-dwelling condominiums (i.e., more than one dwelling per condominium unit), and projects within coastal barriers as designated by the Department of Interior coastal barrier resource maps (Atlantic Ocean, Gulf of Mexico, and the Great Lakes).

Passing the certification requirements can be a challenge, but should be attainable for most condominiums, although the reader should review current requirements since they may have changed since the publication of this book. In that regard, diligence and good business practices are the keys to meeting FHA certification requirements. The appropriate Housing and Urban Development (HUD) jurisdictional Homeownership Center must be contacted and supplied with the required information and documentation to start the certification process. The following is a summary of some of the basic requirements that apply to most condominium projects as of 2012:

• Owner Occupancy Requirement – at least 50 percent of the units must be occupied by the co-owners who own the unit.

• FHA Cap – no more than 50 percent of the condominium units in a condominium project can be FHA insured. (This cap can be increased up to 100 percent if certain additional criteria are met.)

- Investor Ownership Limit – no more than 10 percent of the overall units maybe owned by one investor. In condominium projects containing 10 or fewer units, an investor may not own more than one unit.

- Delinquency Cap – no more than 50 percent of the total units can be in arrears over sixty (60) days. (If warranted pursuant to certain specific FHA criteria, the FHA may permit up to 20 percent delinquencies.)

There are very specific insurance requirements for achieving FHA certification, which should be attainable for a well-administered condominium project with state-of-the-art condominium documents (i.e., Bylaws, Master Deed, etc.). First, proof of liability insurance in a minimum amount of $1,000,000 is required. A copy of the hazard insurance policy demonstrating coverage over all common elements in the condominium project equal to 100 percent current replacement costs must be supplied. An employee dishonesty policy (also known as fidelity bond/insurance) must be provided for all condominium projects containing 20 or more units in an amount equal to three months aggregate assessments plus the amount of the reserve fund. The manager of the condominium must also be covered by the employee dishonesty policy. Unit co-owners must also procure and maintain standard "walls-in" H0-6 insurance policies on their condominium units. Lastly, each condominium project must submit proof of its geographic proximity to a 100-year floodplain in the form of a Federal Emergency Management Agency (FEMA) map. Proof of flood insurance is required if the condominium project is located within a 100-year floodplain. Incidentally, meeting the FHA requirements are beneficial to the association regardless of whether FHA certification is sought or not.

A financial analysis is one of the most significant aspects of the review process pursuant to which the "risk" level of a condominium project is weighed by the FHA. The FHA reviews the financial package to determine if the condominium project meets its financial review standards; specifically, 1) if the allocations and line items are sufficient to maintain and preserve all amenities; 2) if the reserve fund for capital expenditures and deferred maintenance is in an amount equal to at least 10 percent of the budget; and 3) if there is adequate funding to cover the insurance premium(s) and deductible(s). The financial package submitted with the application must contain the following records:

• Current Budget

• Current Balance Sheet

• Income and Expense Statement

If the financial analysis by the FHA determines that the condominium project does not meet its financial review standards, a reserve study less than 24 months old may be requested in order to further assess the financial stability of the condominium project.

UPDATING YOUR CONDOMINIUM DOCUMENTS TO STREAMLINE THE PROCESS

Other documentation required for the certification review by the FHA includes a complete set of the condominium documents, such as the Master Deed (also known as a declaration in some states), the bylaws (both condominium bylaws and corporate bylaws), the condominium subdivision plan (usually exhibit B to the Master Deed), the articles of incorporation for the condominium association, any rules and regulations, and any other documents that are a part of and/or referenced as exhibits to the other condominium documents. It is important to have your condominium documents critiqued by your condominium attorney to determine if they are in compliance with state law, governmental regulations, and other federal and local laws affecting condominiums before submitting them for FHA certification. Among other requirements, the condominium documents must be free of restrictions that prevent the free transfer of property. Also, if your condominium documents contain a "right of first refusal" provision, you may be asked to confirm that it is not applied in a discriminatory manner as prohibited by the Fair Housing Act. An amendment to the condominium documents may be necessary to bring the documents into compliance with all requirements prior to submitting the certification application, which might be the necessary impetus to get your documents amended to conform to new laws and practices.

FHA is also interested in analyzing any pending litigation in which the condominium association and/or the members of the board of directors are a party, not including routine foreclosure actions. The information to be supplied must include the reason for the litigation, anticipated completion date, applicability of any insurance coverage, the impact on future solvency of the condominium association, any impediment to the transfer of title, and/or any impact on co-owner's rights.

Special assessments are also scrutinized by the FHA. Any submission must include an explanation of pending special assessments, including the purpose of the assessment, any impact on unit marketability, a history of special assessments levied at the condominium project, the due date(s), and the impact of the special assessment on the overall financial stability, future value, and marketability of the condominium project.

Since the FHA requirements are promulgated under the authority and jurisdiction of federal law (i.e., the United States Code), the consequences of knowingly and willfully providing untruthful or inaccurate documentation or information include a penalty of a monetary fine and/or imprisonment. Thus, it is imperative that the information and documentation submitted to FHA for the certification process be truthful and accurate, and that the condominium association recognizes that there is a continuing obligation to notify FHA if any material information upon which it relied to grant project-wide certification is no longer true or accurate. Also required is the submission of a certification signed by an authorized representative of the condominium association stating that the condominium project meets all state, local, and FHA approval requirements; that the information and statements made in the application package are true to the best of his or her knowledge and belief; and that the applicant has no knowledge of circumstances or conditions that may have an adverse effect upon the condominium project or cause a mortgage to become delinquent.

It is important to note that the FHA certification requirements can vary depending on a variety of factors unique to each condominium project, including, without limitation, the type of condominium project, the number of units in the condominium, the value of the condominium units, the stage of completion of construction of new condominium projects, and other factors. Somewhat different or additional criteria apply to condominium projects that are under construction and the control of the developer, including the submission of a Phase I Environmental Site Assessment report. You should consult your condominium attorney to determine which requirements pertain to your unique condominium project.

RECERTIFY EVERY TWO YEARS

The FHA review process initially takes about 30 days, after which the applicant is notified of the approval or rejection of the project for certification, or a request is made for additional documentation and/or information from the applicant. Once a condominium project has obtained FHA certification, unit mortgages are eligible to be insured by the FHA. Every two years the FHA certification expires, and the condominium project must go through a re-certification process. Recertification can be started six months prior to expiration and/or be requested up to six months after expiration.

In summary, if the condominium project is the type of project that is eligible for FHA certification, there is likely no good reason not to seek to obtain FHA certification, which should greatly enhance the marketability of the condominium units. If the condominium project does not meet some of the FHA criteria, such as the delinquencies being over 15% of the total units, this may mean that the condominium association needs to step-up its administration of the project to be more effective in running the condominium like a business. Other FHA criteria, such as the financial stability of the condominium project, are more subjective and may be a point of contention that the condominium association may be able to successfully convince the FHA to view more favorably. In any event, every eligible condominium association should strive to meet the FHA criteria and should attempt to obtain FHA certification. It may also be found by a court that the board of directors has a legal and fiduciary responsibility to seek FHA certification for the benefit of its members.

PART III Sound Advice

Now you know a lot more about buying, selling, and operating a condominium and the attendant association. But there are always pitfalls. Here are a few more words of wisdom.

THE
GURU
IS IN

CHAPTER 17

Words of Wisdom
Final Thoughts and "Meisner's Maxims" on Condo Living

Anyone associated with condominiums has a vested interest in seeing to it that this important and pervasive type of housing is successful. Some day, you may sell your home or move from your apartment into a condominium. You may live in a condominium as your first residence. You may dream of a second home, probably a condominium, in a warm, beautiful place. You may buy a condominium as an investment or a residence for your son or daughter during their college years.

That problems in condominium living exist will not be a revelation to anyone who has lived in a condominium. In fact, the word has probably gotten out about what it's really like to live in a condo from my first book. Even *The New York Times* has discussed how the board of directors of condominium associations may spend hours debating the paint color on mail boxes or whether the management company should be able to charge time to come to meetings.

Government intervention alone is not the answer. I was an outspoken opponent when deregulation occurred in Michigan. Nevertheless, I do not believe that absolute government regulation is appropriate.

Ultimately, government cannot regulate every aspect of condominium operation. Admittedly, in the past I have encouraged the close regulation of condo developers. I still believe that the regulation of condominium development could be enhanced through closer scrutiny of the condominium documents and sales documents prepared by developers and their attorneys.

Conversely, the operational structure of the condominium association, once turned over to the members, should be relatively free from government intervention. Sure, there ought to be statutes relating to how associations pursue claims against the developer or co-owners, including rights to seek and recover attorney fees and costs. There also ought to be guarantees of basic co-owner rights when confronted by an aggressive or abusive condo association. Generally, however, the operation of the condo board should be *laissez-faire*.

A PROPOSED SOLUTION

There continues to be a potentially bright future for condos. Whether that future will be marred by the problems such as those discussed in this book may depend on whether steps are taken to improve their operational structure and to educate the public more fully concerning their proper operation. I hope that the perceptions, conclusions, and cynicisms expressed in this second edition are received, reviewed, digested, crystallized, and transformed into energized and directed momentum toward better condominium governance.

What continues to be clear is that the present structure of condominium operation by volunteer board members who have been drafted or coerced, or who are obsessed with power, must be radically changed. Again, I hope that this book will elicit comment and stir controversy, since there needs to be a broad-based discussion of the operation of condo associations. Those involved in condo association operation should applaud such an examination. While there may be differences of opinion as to how best to improve condominium association operation, there can be little disagreement that improvement is still needed and in demand.

A new structure of condominium management should be considered. Board members must be more professionalized. Perhaps a professional chief executive officer (someone from the outside) should assist in the operation of the condo. Politics should be discouraged. Power politics should be eliminated, if that were possible.

All parties need a better understanding of the enabling documents that regulate condo associations and community associations by its leaders. This is not to suggest that they must be condo lawyers, but it will require them to take time and make the effort to improve the condo documents. Directors must understand their role in the community association and the legal relationship between the condo association, its members, the developer, the management agent, the local municipality, and any state condominium regulatory body. Notwithstanding the inherent reluctance of co-owners to do so, directors should be encouraged to spend money on the necessary items discussed in this book.

State and local governments should encourage board member and management consultant education as a condition to participation in the leadership of a condo association. Hopefully, it will not be necessary for the government to legislate mandatory education of directors, management consultants, and the like, although the certification and licensure of management companies is sorely needed.

It also would be helpful if condominium purchasers were better informed before and when they became members of an association. The purchaser of a condominium must have access to accurate information that will lead to reasonable expectations. This starts with a crackdown on those developers and advertisers who paint an erroneous and unrealistic picture of condo living. The real estate broker who solicits customers for condos also must portray what the purchaser reasonably may expect from the condominium milieu. Before they buy, purchasers should be encouraged to read books such as this and to seek the advice of legal counsel to know what they are buying and assuming.

If the volunteer association board is to be maintained, board continuity could be enhanced by requiring that the terms of directors be staggered, and that competent support staff be recruited to assist the board in making decisions. Personality clashes can be avoided by an enlightened electorate that gets to know potential candidates for the board before electing them. Being on the board ought not to be either a door prize or a booby prize, nor should it be bestowed on the person solely because he or she has expressed an interest at an annual meeting. Hopefully, apathy will wane when association members realize their financial investment is at risk and their unwillingness to appreciate, encourage, or become capable candidates undermines their own investment. While the elimination of Nazi-like members from the board or management company cannot be guaranteed, when this personality type appears, the board members should be able to stymie their attempts to exert their will to the detriment of the association. Forceful leadership is good. Autocratic rule is not!

Condos have left their mark on society! Condos also have left their mark on the people involved in them. I have frequently been told by people who live in condos that they will never do it again. I have sometimes uttered that pronouncement myself. In one of my recent management classes, I was reminded by a co-owner of a condo that his priest still will not let the condominium association hold a meeting in his church, 10 years after he was forced to evict its unruly members from the church hall. I find that not only to be incredible, but also rather sorrowful. Perhaps it's a harbinger of the direction in which many condos have gone and will go unless necessary improvements are implemented. Hopefully, some of the ideas, thoughts and concerns that this book explores will have a therapeutic and constructive effect on those who are willing to take the time to both read and digest its contents. My first edition evoked that response, and I have every reason to believe that this revised and expanded edition will do so also.

MEISNER'S MAXIMS

Over the years I have developed notions and idiosyncrasies, some obviously cynical, concerning patterns of conduct and common scenarios that occur in dealing with condominium boards and community associations in general. What follows are affectionately and proudly entitled (tongue in cheek) "Meisner's Maxims." These postulates have not been empirically tested. But chances are, if you ever have any experience in dealing with a condominium or community association, you will encounter them at some time.

If readers have their own maxims of condo operation, feel free to send them to the address listed in the References section. I will be happy to consider their inclusion in yet another sequel to this book or on our webpage.

MEISNER'S MAXIM NO. 1

"A decision of a condominium governing body is not equal to the sum of the individual opinions shared by its members."

Those who are well-versed in algebra will no doubt take me to task regarding Meisner's Maxim No. 1, but I believe that it is true. Boards make decisions rather whimsically, and the group decision often is not a composite of the individual opinions of the individual board members. Chances are that if you polled the board on a decision that was made by the whole group, the individual opinions of board members would not add up to the decision made by the board.

What I am suggesting is that board members make compromises, change their feelings, are intimidated, and in some cases simply don't care about issues that come before them. They may have individual opinions but go along with either the "group" or the lead of the member who usurps power and imposes his or her will on the rest of the board. This phenomenon often results in illogical and inane decisions by boards who have failed to think through the ramifications of their decisions.

MEISNER'S MAXIM NO. 2

"Behind every board member is a person(s) pulling a string."

This maxim is analogous to the notion that our politicians do not act for themselves, but are merely the servants of special interest groups. In the condominium context, the "special interest group" may be the spouse, live-in friend or mother of the board member, or perhaps his "fishing buddy" who lives across the street. Board members have friends, relatives, in-laws, and business partners who live in or have a financial interest in the condominium. He or she wants to serve the needs of his "constituents," and when his string is pulled, the board member reacts. It's reality in the dynamics of condominium operation and, presumably, many other groups, including, of course, our politicians.

MEISNER'S MAXIM NO. 3

"Even when it's too hot in the kitchen, certain board members won't get out."

Board membership is a thankless task which one may expect to require the substantial expenditure of time and, more often than not, to result in criticism. Although not everyone is cut out to serve on a board, there are some people who just don't realize that they are among them, even when they are elected or appointed to the board. They may appreciate the complexity of the job, but they really don't have the time or ability to handle it. Regardless of whether they are doing a competent job, these directors are like fixtures whose lights may dim, but are never replaced. They go on and on, making little or no contribution, and end up being revered, believe it or not, by those naive souls in the condominium who respect longevity. After all, if you've been there long enough, you must know what you are doing!

MEISNER'S MAXIM NO. 4

"Spend as little money as possible ... at whatever potential cost."

Some directors will, no doubt, have the perception that they should be as penurious as possible, at whatever potential cost. They do not care whether the association gets proper legal advice, for they will somehow make the decisions on their own or will rely on the managing agent's free "legal advice." They will not retain a landscape contractor because one of the retired persons at the condo cuts the grass. They will not fund any money for reserves since they'd rather have the money in their own pockets. They will go to small claims court to save the association the money it costs to have an attorney file a lien and pursue effective legal action, even though the association has a good chance to recoup that money from the delinquent co-owner including all of their legal fees and costs in a court of record. Their contribution to the members of the association, they believe, is that they have done everything they can do to avoid spending money. If things get screwed up, they can always say to neighbors, "Hey, I saved you money and you didn't have to pay me for it!" (Of course, those neighbors also got what they paid for and may turn around and sue them.)

MEISNER'S MAXIM NO. 5

"What has been learned will be forgotten, ignored, or placed in purgatory."

The directors and officers of condo associations are generally not students of history. They frequently do not learn from their mistakes or the mistakes of past boards. They ignore their past experiences and contradict themselves, sometimes merely for the sake of contradicting themselves. Often, the same people aren't around to learn from prior experiences or from those who preceded them. Often, new people coming on the board don't want to know what the previous board has done or experienced because they think that the new board should "make a fresh start." But then, of course, we have directors who are serving on the board for a second time and want to correct what they did the first time!

In short, this maxim holds that stagnation and circuity are rampant. The board revolves in circles (sometimes taking seven to ten years to complete a revolution) and then starts again at the beginning—except that the condo development has depreciated without any real progress being made.

MEISNER'S MAXIM NO. 6
"If you want to win friends and influence people, don't live in a condominium ... and don't serve on its board."

There are, of course, some directors of condominiums who will do whatever is possible to satisfy everyone at the condo, which, of course, they cannot hope to do. They believe that, in the residential context, they should be as pleasant as possible to their neighbors. These people won't last long on the condo board because their neighbors will eat them up, either by disregarding the restrictions or imposing their will.

On the other hand, there are some directors who do whatever they please because they don't care what their neighbors think. They may be egotistical or narcissistic, and may recognize that serving on the board is their chance to dominate someone else. They won't be able to dominate everyone, and they may get beat up themselves, psychologically and sometimes physically.

No, the best thing for those who want to win friends and

influence people is to stay out of association affairs. In fact, if you want to win friends and influence people, don't get involved in a condominium in the first place. If you buy a condo, you are going to be encouraged to serve on the board. That's the best way to lose friends.

It's like becoming president of the United States or a circuit judge. It's different when you are up there—you look at your friends or lawyer peers (and they look at you) differently. There is a transformation from someone who is perceived as civil and rational to someone who is engulfed in the group dynamics of neighbors engaged in self-management of community affairs or directing lawyers. You are better off buying a farmhouse or even living in an apartment where the only controlling person you have to deal with is the landlord!

MEISNER'S MAXIM NO. 7

"He who works best, works least."

This is a curious maxim in that it goes against the Protestant work ethic (now a minority) that is the backbone of American capitalism. The truth is that in condominium associations, the board members try to do all the work and, generally, the work is not completed or done well in such condominiums. Simply put, the directors are not merely making policy decisions but also are trying to carry out the policy decisions themselves.

You probably have seen it if you have lived in a condominium. The directors cut the grass, paint the complex, and grab you by the arm, warning you that you cannot walk your dog and allow it to defecate on the condominium common elements. No, the best directors are ones who work the least, who delegate their tasks to people who are experienced in carrying out the preroga-tives and policies of the board—management companies, accoun-tants, insurance consultants, attorneys, and the like. These directors go to their board meetings and make policies, but they aren't shoveling the snow or generating unnecessary heat.

MEISNER'S MAXIM NO. 8

"Liberty and the pursuit of happiness are unconstitutional."

Lest you think for one minute that your condominium association is a democracy and that you are entitled to due process, equal protection of the laws, and happiness, buy a condo and live there for a time! As soon as you receive a dunning letter from the association that threatens to cut off your utilities because you have been slow in paying your assessments, you will not be happy. As soon as you receive a letter that your dog has been observed to have pooped in too many places, or that you parked your car in the visitor parking spot, you are going to feel that you are being harassed.

Why can't you put up the American flag on your front lawn? Because the board has told you that it is an exterior modification for which you need the board's written approval, which is denied because the board doesn't like the size of the stars on your flag. (Indeed, in Michigan and by the U.S. Code they had to pass a statute allowing a co-owner to display the American flag on the exterior of his unit.) Moreover, as they will point out to you, they have a right to enforce the condo documents, and when you bought the condominium, you agreed to adhere to the restrictions, rules, and regulations.

The lawyer for the condo association even points out to you that there is case law to the effect that when you buy a condominium, you inherently give up certain liberties that you would have in other types of housing. You can't refute that proposition, but somehow you think it's not right. But it is right, because that's the reality of condo living.

If you want to be happy, as the song goes, "Be Happy," but probably in some other type of residential setting. Don't forget, if you breach the condominium restrictions after a judge orders you to comply, you could "go to jail" without "passing Go."

MEISNER'S MAXIM NO. 9

"Shakespeare was right in saying 'kill the lawyers,' but wait until the lawsuit is completed."

Now there is one area where all condominium co-owner agree. They may disagree on the company that should pick up the garbage, or on whether the assessment should be increased to build an addition to the pool, or on whether it is right to allow non-residents to participate in Mahjong parties in the clubhouse. But all will agree that there is no useful purpose for lawyers in the condominium or, for that matter, in society as a whole, and they will do what they can to do without lawyers. They will generally come to that conclusion, if not before, but after they have been compelled to use a lawyer, presumably in a lawsuit, after which they will, no doubt, figuratively "kill the lawyer!"

Under this maxim, it does not matter whether the lawyer has prevailed in the lawsuit. If the lawyer charges the association for his services, the maxim requires that he be terminated. The maxim requires that in a condominium, all co-owners who have had to pay assessments to the association and also, perhaps, special assessments for legal fees, must join in at the association's annual meeting in singing "let's kill the S.O.B." and not pay his estate!

MEISNER'S MAXIM NO. 10

"In any condo hierarchy, an individual will fall to his level of incompetence."

At the risk of offending Lawrence Peter (the founder of the "Peter Principle"), although the Peter Principle may apply to the person who is elevated to a position on a condominium association board with responsibilities that he is incapable of handling, we also have the antithesis. The person who is well skilled in his other endeavors falls to a common level of incompetence as soon as he joins the condo's board of directors. The typical example of this phenomenon is the prominent corporate executive or physician who abandons his training, background, experience, and common sense and gets into fights with other board members, fails to support the spending of necessary funds , and reverts to social gathering or country club behavior—i.e., he avoids at all cost "stepping on the neighbors' toes." He, therefore, becomes an ineffectual director and meekly descends to the lowest common denominator of the board, the village drunk.

MEISNER'S MAXIM NO. 11
"Time shrinks to do work."

Parkinson's Law says that "work expands to fill the time available for its completion," and, consequently, directors will make work for themselves or create controversy to satisfy a need or void in their life. Unfortunately, the antithesis is also true: There is no time for doing the work of the condo when one serves on a board.

Complacency, apathy, and the notion that condo living is "carefree living" permeate the attitudes of board members. Once on the board, directors determine that they don't have time to deal with the problems or do the work attendant to their office. They don't have the time to learn about fiduciary duties. They don't have the time to read or understand the condo documents. They don't have the time to develop necessary skills. In short, whatever goes on is undertaken by the person who has allowed his work to expand to fill his time. One or two people do all the work, and the other board members do little or nothing.

MEISNER'S MAXIM NO. 12
"If something can go wrong in the condominium, it will."

This maxim is, admittedly, an offshoot of Murphy's Law, adapted to condominiums. You will recall from Murphy's Law that, if something can go wrong, it will. Well, in condos if something can go wrong, it not only will, it will be worse than any place else, perhaps resulting in litigation and/or a special assessment.

A further corollary to this maxim is that, for years to come, neither the board of directors nor the co-owners may realize what has gone wrong. Generally, it will take a new purchaser who is so offended by the conduct of the board of directors that he gets stirred up. If that co-owner has some business law background or is an advocate of civil rights, he may confront the board. All hell may break loose if the board is confronted by this "recalcitrant" co-owner over policies of the board of directors that have been meekly accepted by the other co-owners for many years, even though these policies have been spawned in mediocrity, illegality, or non-logic.

MEISNER'S MAXIM NO. 13

"The 'Golden Rule' is too expensive to follow in a condominium."

Most condo owners, if asked if they believe in the Golden Rule, would answer that they do. That is, that they should treat their neighbor the same way they would like to be treated.

Of course, that maxim is much too costly in a condominium. There are directors who perceive that priorities must be set regarding the condo operations, particularly concerning maintenance and repair items. The truth in a condo is that repairs will be made to some roofs, but not to others. Concessions will be made to certain co-owners, but not to others. Modifications will be allowed to some co-owners, but not to others. Assessments will be collected from some co-owners, but not from others. All of this is because, in the condominium, uniform treatment and equal treatment are not widely practiced, and it's just too expensive. Plus, it is hard to be fair and keep board members from receiving special dispensation.

MEISNER'S MAXIM NO. 14

"The more things change on the board of directors, the worse they get!"

An irrefutable axiom in condo operation is that when new

directors come on the board, they feel they must redo and undo everything that previously has taken place. The change is generally manifested by a desire to replace the management company, the insurance agent, or the lawyer (particularly if they can find a cheaper one). The upshot is that new people are brought in who, together with these new directors, must grapple with the learning process. Policies that were set by previous boards are dismantled or forgotten. Old ideas are pushed aside.

The board tries to reinvent the wheel. In a condo operation, frequently that's exactly what happens. Many times, depending on the caliber of the board elected, the wheel comes out square the first six months to a year and never turns smoothly again.

MEISNER'S MAXIM NO. 15
"The more affluent the condo, the cheaper the condo."

Some readers won't grasp this concept or be willing to accept it, at least initially. Nevertheless, those of us who have had experience with condos—and with people who have attained a certain level of wealth—have come to appreciate that financial success does not guarantee that one will be more enlightened, generous, or businesslike.

To the contrary, and rather remarkably so, the more affluent a condominium association, the more penurious (cheap) that association may be. Certainly, the tendency of the co-owners toward arrogance, enlarged egos, and inflated perception of knowledge and intelligence also make it difficult to represent the affluent condominium. But frankly, they're always looking for a deal. They don't pay retail for anything—and sometimes they just don't pay, period!

No doubt you've run across these people in your experiences. While they seem to gravitate toward an organizational structure, they don't want to spend money on lawyers and, in fact, they're scared to death to pay lawyer's fees. Doctors are generally the most notorious, followed closely by engineers and lawyers themselves. You would think that the more affluent condos, at least, would be more able and willing to spend money on the essentials necessary to run the association properly. Not true! They spend little or no money, perhaps because they perceive themselves to be experts, or perhaps because their ex-wife's divorce lawyer "ripped them off," an experience which caused them to develop a general disdain for lawyers.

Such people may be the most difficult to organize because they all have their own perceptions of how the association should operate and are looking out for their own interests. A community atmosphere is generally less prevalent in the more affluent condos because the co-owners tend to be more individualized, preoccupied with their diverse interests and, often, downright selfish.

Of course, what's affluent is relative. Undoubtedly, it is dependent on the geographical location in which you live. To some, an affluent condominium may be any condominium where the unit price is more than $250,000. Others may think an affluent condominium is any condominium in which the units are in the $750,000 price range. But you'll recognize what I consider to be an affluent condo when you see the composition of its co-owners. I'm not talking about upper price scale condos. I'm talking about condos where the people are basically multimillionaires. Watch out in that setting!

MEISNER'S MAXIM NO. 16
"Never, under any circumstances, hire a lawyer when you should without first exhausting every possible dead end."

For some reason, condominium boards think legal advice and/ or assistance will come from God, heaven, some other terrestrial being, the building inspector, the state legislator, the U.S. congressman, the U.S. senator, and/or the Chinese Communists. Boards for whatever reason will gravitate to whatever forum they think may provide them with free advice irrespective of whether the persons from whom they seek advice are capable, competent, and ready or are willing to provide such advice, all in an effort to save legal fees. This is obviously bad for the reasons outlined in this book!

MEISNER'S MAXIM NO. 17

"When you first don't succeed, give up until you are thrown out of office."

Now we all know that directors of community associations are volunteers who serve without compensation and generally without appreciation. Their motivation, then, to do the right job is guarded because they don't want to offend anyone, even if it takes disregarding the need to raise assessments, build up reserves, take affirmative action against delinquent or recalcitrant co-owners, or sue the developer who is a former friend of theirs. In fact, whenever there is a dead end presented, they say, "Thank God Almighty, because I don't have to do anything else." They never question the fact that taking no for an answer sometimes is not the best thing to do given the ability of the board to exercise political and legal power to deal with the issues that come before the association, and that there may be creative ways to get the problem resolved even if you first don't succeed.

MEISNER'S MAXIM NO. 18

"Make sure that all of the people in the condominium expect to do their own job working to maintain and clean up the place no matter what their physical or mental state because it saves money."

Now we all know that associations are notoriously penurious and want to spend as little money at whatever cost. What this means, of course, is that even though many co-owners bought their condominium thinking they would have carefree living, what it really means is that there will be pressure brought on them to cut their own grass, paint the exterior of their unit, donate chairs to the clubhouse, rake the leaves, and maintain the financial books. Anything but to hire a professional management company and/or appropriate contractors that cost too much money for the association. Of course, what they don't realize is that these people can sue the association if they are hurt (for which the association may not have adequate insurance coverage); and if there is defective work performed, it ends up being that the association must sue one of its own, perhaps a director or co-owner contractor, for malfeasance or negligence, which exacerbates an already bad situation.

MEISNER'S MAXIM NO. 19

"If you want to impeach your association's board of directors because it levied a special assessment, things will not get peachier financially."

It is likely that the board of directors, under great pressure, levied an additional or special assessment only because the association needed the money. Often that evokes anger on the part of the co-owners, who don't like paying taxes or condominium assessments no matter what the need. If the assessment doesn't go through, the association will be in for even greater problems.

MEISNER'S MAXIMS NO. 20

"Terrorists in condos are usually frustrated former CFOs who got squeezed out of their jobs and now want to put the squeeze on necessary expenditures and play financial wiz."

Just because somebody was a CFO of a corporation doesn't mean he or she has any knowledge about fiscal responsibility for an association. This includes the need to spend money and take chances on occasion in regard to litigation and other matters—not necessarily from a cost benefit standpoint, but from an understanding of what the long-term ramifications could be if the association does not, for example, enforce a bylaw restriction.

MEISNER'S MAXIM NO. 21

"If a smooth-talking maritime lawyer on your board boasts that he can lead your association out of its legal issues with the developer, better get a life raft before the condo sinks."

There are directors who for their own egotistical purposes, particularly if they are lawyers, will command more respect and/ or allegiance from the members of the association even if those persons are not operating in good faith, have their own agenda, or frankly don't know what they are talking about. I have seen leaders of community associations who are deceptive and out-and-out liars to the members of their association by leading them down the unfortunate primrose path of litigation or non-litigation.

MEISNER'S MAXIMS NO. 22

"There is safety in numbers unless your condo lawyer accumulated too many bones on which to chew based on his time and/or resources."

Some community association lawyers brag about how many associations they represent. While that may be a good marketing tool, it is also important to determine whether that attorney has the resources, including lawyers and trained legal assistants, to handle the volume of work that he has accumulated. It may be that he has accumulated that business based on marketing skills whereby lowballing his charges and/or being in bed with management companies who continuously refer him business because they know they will never have a problem with him representing the association against them, if any issue arises.

MEISNER'S MAXIM NO. 23

"It is never too late to learn, unless you are on a board of directors of affluent braggarts."

If you've got affluent braggarts on your board, or any type of braggart for that matter, no matter what you say or no matter how you articulate your concerns, that person will not change their thinking. What you will learn from that experience is that some people will not listen to reason if they have their own agenda, are abrasive, or are former psychologists.

MEISNER'S MAXIMS NO. 24

"If your rental management company is only charging you a 75 percent commission on vacation rentals, they haven't ripped you off enough."

We have been in a number of cases involving excessive charges by rental management companies for the renting of recreational condominium units. We have even had cases where the rental agreement was set aside and/or deemed to be unenforceable. It is best, as always, to determine whether the rental agreement is enforceable and whether or not you can get a better deal from a competent rental management company and/or whether the association can be of any assistance in assuring that rentals are handed out among out the units equally and properly.

CONCLUSION

Whenever people live in close proximity, someone is bound to eventually leave the cap off the toothpaste. As the late Rodney King said: "Can we all just get along?"

Meisner's Maxims are not likely to serve as a substitute for the Ten Commandments, the Declaration of Independence or, for that matter, the state condominium enabling statute. Rather, they are intended only as a source of reference from which the reader may draw certain conclusions regarding the reality of living in a condominium.

If these maxims evoke controversy ... wonderful! If they encourage a professional analysis of condominium living ... great (except, of course, to the extent that there may be a desire to kill lawyers)! And if these maxims cause you to chuckle ... enjoy!

CHAPTER 18

Ask the Gurus
Newspaper Columns and
Anecdotes from Legal Beagles

I have been fortunate enough to be author of a real estate column for more than 35 years concentrating on community association matters, but also dealing with other issues that come up in the real estate field. While I have literally authored more than a thousand real estate queries, I have attempted to take a small cross-section of these columns from the *Observer & Eccentric* newspapers to include in my book so the reader can have a better insight into some of the issues in real estate that may not have been touched upon in this book. I encourage all of you to read my column and submit questions, which I will to attempt answer in a concise and comprehensive fashion.

Q: Our managing agent finally admitted upon inquiry that our attorney has done work for him on a personal basis and never disclosed that to the board until specific questions were asked. The agent vehemently stands behind our attorney as someone who can do a good job. What do you think?

A: *That may well be the case, but the managing agent should disclose any relationships of a business or personal nature with any persons with whom the association does business, including this attorney. Ask that if there is a problem between the association's managing agent and the attorney, would the attorney be willing to pursue the managing agent on behalf of the association or, for that matter, even "spill the beans" on the managing agent because of their relationship. If he says no, perhaps you need a new attorney and a new management company.*

Q: The president of our condominium association has been charged with a felony. It occurred in the parking lot of our condominium. The victim is a member of our community and has signed an intent to prosecute. We have also had other problems with the president as far as conflict of interest, improper bids, and other criminal charges currently on file. Can our community and/or board be sued for his actions, and if the victim is awarded damages and medical costs, can the members' property be attached for payment?

A: *This is, of course, a difficult question, which is very fact-intensive. But if the other directors were aware of the president's problems and they did nothing, then they may be a part of the problem and potentially liable. In a sense, responsibility could also be placed on the members in that they elected him as a director. However, whether they have personal liability as members is another matter. Since the other directors elected him as president and did not control the situation, they could become liable. In any event, you are best advised to consult with your attorney and your insurance carrier as soon as possible.*

Q: Our association has a judgment against the bank for non-payment of assessments. Our lawyer seems to be too busy to handle the matter and says that eventually the bank will pay. What do you suggest?

A: *I suggest that if you have exhausted your efforts to resolve the matter amicably with the bank, you get a lawyer to execute on the bank by literally getting a sheriff to go to the bank and, if necessary, remove desk computers, copiers, filing cabinets, and any cash in the teller's drawers. That will clearly send the bank a message. We have also, on occasion, had to get the sheriff to go to a liquor store in order to seize merchandise in order to satisfy a judgment against the owner. When the judgment debtor is not willing to cooperate, you have a right to avail yourself of all legal means to collect the amount owing.*

Q: We are getting a home warranty from our seller, and I am wondering whether or not that is going to protect us with respect to problems that have come up in the condominium.

A: *It may or may not, as there has been much discourse regarding the adequacy of home warranties and the unwillingness on the part of many home warranty companies to replace rather than repair an item. In checking out the type of warranty you are getting, find out, obviously, who is giving the warranty, and find out exactly what the contract covers and how much the service fee is. For example, pools, spa tubs, and other specialty items might not be included. Also check to see whether the company has policies on pre-existing conditions and whether those repairs would be covered. Find out how the company handles complaints about the contractors who handle repairs, and ask whether the company will let you buy a new appliance or item at a reduced rate if you would rather have it replaced than repaired. In short, a warranty is only as good as the company behind it—and the language that is used in the warranty agreement itself. Get your real estate lawyer specialist to review the warranty as part of a review of your purchase agreement before you sign on the dotted line, and always include a lawyer review contingency in the purchase agreement.*

Q: What if my condominium association's officers refuse to do an audit? I am trying to sell my place but I cannot do it because there are no audits and no lawyer would recommend to their client to get into such a mess.

A: *The Michigan Condominium Act requires that an audit be provided on an annual basis by an independent accountant. More than likely, your bylaws also require at least that type of an undertaking. The fact that your association has refused to do so is gross mismanagement, and your lawyer, if you have one, should write a letter advising the board of the fact that they are in violation of the Condominium Act, and it is impeding your ability to sell your unit with consequential damages suffered by you.*

Q: Is it a good idea to have a husband and wife on the board of our condominium?

A: *I must respond by saying that it "proverbially" all depends. First, the documents have to allow that both the husband and wife, being presumably joint owners of the condominium, have the right to individually serve on the board. Secondly, the potential husband and wife team must recognize that it could create strife internally in their family. Also, it may create the impression that one family is "running the show" so to speak, and it may create ill will. On the other hand, if the husband and wife were elected by the populace, one can always argue that it was the co-owners' decision to allow them to serve on the board jointly. Sometimes, because of necessity and/or apathy, it is necessary to get a level-headed board member, and it may end up being the spouse of one of the present directors. In short, it all depends upon the circumstances.*

Q: I am a board member of a large condominium, and our attorney says that if there is no equity in the unit, there is no point in going after the co-owner for delinquencies. He also boasts about representing hundreds of condominium associations, but we are never able to get ahold of him and he has a *laissez-faire* attitude toward us. Now, is he correct?

A: *Each case has to be evaluated on its own merits. Many times, even though there is not equity in the unit for the association to obtain payment, there are alternate means of recovery, including getting a personal judgment against the delinquent co-owners and seeking to recover the judgment through garnishment, execution, and the like. Moreover, depending on the situation, the association may have a right to take priority, vis-à-vis the mortgage company, in terms of the equity in the unit. It sounds like your attorney is too busy or too brazen to give you the service that you need, and you are best advised to seek new counsel.*

Q: What do we do with someone who is hoarding all kinds of junk in their condominium unit, including a situation that is causing mold, animal waste, vermin, and a potential fire hazard?

A: *It is, of course, a difficult problem, but most of the time your condominium documents allow for recourse by the association. Obviously, you need to identify the problem and the association's obligation, if any, to deal with it. You need to request access for a board representative and an outside expert to view the problem. You need to deliver the scope to the co-owner and give them a date certain to have the place cleared out or restored, if applicable. Upon the co-owner's failure to remove the stuff and restore it, if applicable by the date certain, after notice to the co-owner, the association's expert should have the stuff removed and the work done, if at all possible, upon the advice of counsel. If you need an injunctive order from the court, you will have to start a lawsuit. You may also want to consider contacting local social service agencies to determine whether or not there is a psychological problem with the co-owner. Obviously, if the owner does not remove the materials, you may have the right under the documents to do so without liability to the association, its managers, directors, etc. On the other hand, you may have to get an injunctive order and hopefully recover all costs, expenses, and legal fees from the co-owner.*

Q: I am a new treasurer for our site condo association. I don't quite understand the rules/law regarding the 10 percent of the budget that needs to be set aside for the reserve fund. Is that 10 percent per year? So if the total budget is $10,000, does $1,000 get put into the reserve fund once?

A: The Michigan Condominium Act requires that a reserve fund be maintained for major repairs and replacements of common elements in a Michigan condominium, and the Michigan Administrative Code requires that it be at a minimum at least 10 percent of the budget, on a non-cumulative basis. While this means that only 10 percent of the budget is required to be in the fund under the Code, the Federal Housing Administration (FHA) is requiring that each annual budget contain a line item in the minimum amount of 10 percent of the budget. Moreover, the board is required by the Act to reasonably determine how much is needed in reserves. Although a site condominium project is not required to obtain FHA certification for FHA-backed loans, lenders often want to be assured that the FHA requirements are met by the condominium before funding a loan. Your board of directors may be well advised to have a reserve study conducted by a reputable company to ascertain the condition of the common elements to determine how much reserve monies need to be set aside for projected future repairs and replacements. You should consult an experienced condominium attorney to determine if your project and condominium documents meet the applicable legal requirements, standards, and laws.

Q: We are in the process of considering a review of our documents, and some of the co-owners are concerned about additional construction in our site condominium, which would impair their view, but the developer has not provided any type of guarantee. What do you recommend?

A: If your community is located in a scenic area, such as near a beach, lake, or in the city with a famous skyline, the view that co-owners enjoy from their units is, obviously, very important to them. Co-owners often buy their particular units because of the views and are dismayed if they are obscured by a structure or foliage added later. Co-owners that have paid for a specific view that they can no longer enjoy or that previously made their unit more valuable and unique than others, making resale easier, could possibly sue the association or the developer. That is why your association should consider passing a view protection bylaw that prohibits co-owners from building or planning anything that would block other co-owners' views. In order to pass and implement a successful view protection bylaw, your attorney must carve out key rights for your association and clearly define the terms in the bylaw, including:

• *At what point in time a view is "protected," and,*

• *Whether the association must enforce a bylaw that protects the co-owners' right to that view.*

Q: I am renting a condominium from someone who bought a home and cannot sell his condominium, plus I needed a place near my daughter's house. I have been there for almost two years and pay my rent. One of the owners had a plumbing problem and the dues went up $25 a month for all owners to cover the thousands that it cost to do repairs. Am I required to pay the increase in dues?

A: Not necessarily, unless your lease arrangement provides that you have to pay any increase in dues (assessments) to the association. That is, if your rent is based on a flat fee per month, irrespective of the dues (assessments), you have no obligation to pay additional sums. If the landlord tells you otherwise, you ought to consult with an experienced real estate attorney.

Q: Our homeowners love to get in the spirit of the holidays, and our association sponsors a decorating contest, hosts a party in the community center, and uses association funds to adorn common elements. Unfortunately, however, the association party and common area decorations support Christmas. There are residents who support other religions and are complaining that the association isn't doing enough to support their religious beliefs and backgrounds. What do you think?

A: This is a difficult question that may sometimes lead to an issue of religious discrimination. Under federal fair housing laws, it is unlawful to discriminate against any person in "the provision of services or facilities" because of religion, and the law is broadly interpreted. You may wish to have all of the major religions represented in your decorations or make it as non-sectarian as possible. Perhaps a general holiday party policy and decorations that do not provide any implications as to a religious representation would be appropriate, but you are best to consult with your attorney for a legal opinion.

Q: Our association is concerned about using volunteers because of the risks that may be involved. Do you have any suggestions?

A: *When in doubt, check with your insurance agent. Ask the volunteers if they have their own insurance and if they will sign a "hold harmless" agreement drafted by your attorney. Be sure you are getting good volunteers, if, in fact, you choose to use them. Make sure the volunteers have the skills to do the job. Make sure that their work is reviewed through proper oversight, and have a board resolution either authorizing the volunteers to do the work or clarify what type of work cannot be done by volunteers. Everything else being considered, it is probably a good idea not to use volunteers unless you are adequately protected.*

Q: We live in a detached condominium, and every year the board of directors undertakes an exterior inspection of all of the units for maintenance purposes. However, this year we received notice that they are offering an interior/exterior inspection to the interior of the unit, but it would be the financial responsibility of the individual co-owner. Our bylaws state that the association has access to the units as necessary for maintenance, repair, or replacement of any of the common elements and to make emergency repairs to prevent damage to the common elements. However, I feel that an interior inspection is an invasion of my privacy. Would it be within my rights to refuse the interior inspection?

A: *It appears from your question that they are making the interior inspection an option, which you do not have to accept. If that is the case, you can obviously opt not to have an interior inspection. On the other hand, to the extent that the association believes that it needs to inspect your unit for common element problems, I think there is a good argument that the cost should be defrayed by the association. If, on the other hand, the inspec-*

tion of the unit deals with problems that are within the co-own-er's responsibility to maintain repair or replacement, then that is something that should be the co-owner's responsibility. You should determine exactly why and what is going to be the subject matter of any inspection in the interior of your unit and whether it is mandatory or not.

Q: The president of our board wants to know whether we should get involved in endorsing any local candidates for election. Do you have any comments on that?

A: The association, through its board, should, in my judgment, steer clear of endorsing candidates entirely. Endorsing a candidate and coming out on the wrong side of an election could certainly end up doing the association a disservice. The best bet is to make this announcement at a board meeting. Let the co-owners know that the association will not be getting involved in any local politics. Obviously, there may be an unusual issue which directly affects the association like an express train going through the middle of the project where some involvement by the association, either politically or legally, would be required, but that is a rare situation.

Q: Our condominium lawyer has contacted us about a short sale of a unit owner where there are substantial assessments due and owing and wants us to make a substantial compromise of the back assessments. What has been your experience?

A: Obviously, each case depends upon its own facts and circumstances, but generally I advise my community association clients to stand firm with respect to short sales since it is the mortgage company that should bear the brunt of any loss, given the fact that they permitted the loan to be made in the first instance. Perhaps you should get a second opinion from another attorney who is experi-

enced in community association law and who may be best able to negotiate with the seller of the unit on behalf of the association.

Q: I am selling a house and my agent, who also represented the buyer, is making it a profitable resell without disclosure to me on the same house. Does that violate his fiduciary duty?

A: I most certainly think it would, and based on a recent case out of Delaware, the Supreme Court agreed finding that a breach of fiduciary duty by the agent elevating his own interests above those of his principal and failing to disclose that conflict created by the resell arrangement was a breach of fiduciary duty. Moreover, the fact that the agent had gotten a waiver did not shield the agent because he did not act as a dual agent representing the buyer and seller in the same transaction. Instead, in that case, he represented two sellers in two different sales earning a second, higher commission on the second sale which likely caused him to subordinate the first seller's interests to his own. Moreover, the court said that if the owner knew of the intended resell, she could have set a higher price for the house.

LEGAL BEAGLES
CANINE COLUMNISTS WEIGH IN ON DOGGED ISSUES

Bailley, the legal beagle, was born in 2001, and is the head legal beagle with our firm. She not only calms our nerves and brings us joy when she comes to the office, usually on Fridays, but is the author of her own column, excerpts of which follow this introduction. Her comments deal with legal issues affecting canines in all aspects of life and we encourage you to not only read her columns in our book but follow her on our website. Joyleih, born in 2009, is our assistant legal beagle and is learning the ropes through her apprenticeship in our office and writes her own column which is similar to Bailley's, but from a more youthful stance. Her kernels of wisdom can also be found on the following pages and on our website.

BAILLEY'S COMMENTARIES

FUN FOR FIDO

Now as the Legal Beagle involved in community associations, I often sniff through the *Common Ground Magazine* published by the Community Association Institute. Of particular interest was an article on page 55 of the January/February 2012 edition that was entitled "Fun for Fido." In that article, they noted that there were approximately 77.5 million dogs owned in the U.S., and 39 percent of all households own at least one, according to the American Pet Products Manufacturers Association. They go on to say that a "pet-friendly community can mean the difference between a family that moves in and one that moves elsewhere. A dog park can be a huge selling point." The article then goes into talking about the various components that should be considered in putting together a dog park. It shows a picture of a dog, although it is not one of a beautiful beagle, since we are generally the most beautiful of all breeds. I think that it is a great idea, and Mary Helen Sprecher should be applauded for making this suggestion.

PIT BULL SERVICE DOGS

I read about a case in Colorado where a city banned pit bulls, but a disabled resident has a pit bull service dog. I don't particularly like pit bulls, but I know they can be important animals for helping people cope with their problems. I am also aware of the fact that the United States Department of Justice issued final rules regarding banned breed service dogs. These rules, which took effect in March 2011, prohibit dogs from being banned as service dogs because of their breed. Obviously, the people who have pit bulls as service dogs do not want to be imposed with cumbersome restrictions or with the fear that the dog may be taken away by an overzealous animal control officer. I don't particularly like animal control officers, unless I have flown the coop and need a ride home, which is unlikely to be the case because of the soft life that I have living where I do and still being able to earn a dog living as a "Legal Beagle."

DOG THERAPY AT GROUND ZERO

In the *Wall Street Journal* for Saturday/Sunday, Sept. 10-11, 2011, I noted a feature article entitled "Dog Therapy at Ground Zero," which had a picture of a golden retriever named Nikie. Apparently, a gentleman named Frank Shane, a professional dog therapist and CEO of the K-9 Disaster Relief Foundation, had to improvise when he brought Nikie down to Ground Zero shortly after 9/11. There was no protocol for anything from the kind of footwear Nikie would wear to how Frank should deal with the grief of 9/11. He, however, stepped onto the site and the rest was a great camaraderie (I learned that word from Bob) between Nikie and the relief workers at the site. Nikie, on every level, offered a small break from the intensity of the workers at Ground Zero and had full access to even restricted areas. Fortunately, there was a veterinarian protocol that included putting talcum powder in his boots and weighing him every day. He worked eight hour shifts on the site, even more time than I do, but he always had his rest time. The article says that people became "very protective of him," and his trainer did not have to carry a collapsible bowl for Nikie to drink or eat since the others always had food for him wherever he went. Nikie also had a trademark flag scarf that he wore around his neck. His trainer, at the end of their time at the site when everyone went home, was given more than 2,000 flag scarves that were donated to give away to the workers. Just another example of how great we dogs serve in both joyous times and in times of tragedy.

UNLOVED PUPPY MILL DOGS

I love reading *USA Today* because there is always a good column about dogs. The column by Sharon I. Peters that I read was about 23 Italian greyhounds, very thin, watchful, and weary. They had traveled 735 miles from southwest Missouri and had been temporarily housed after state officials seized them from a commercial breeding operation. These so-called puppy mills are despicable, and fortunately Joyleih and I were not conceived in that environment. The article talks about the National Mill Dog Rescue, where on any given day, 150 to 200 dogs of all types are in rehab. Most have landed there after breeders targeted them to be shot, drowned or, in rare cases, euthanized by a vet to make room for more productive breeders. Once they are healthy, they are moved into house pet readiness. This rescue group has saved and adopted out nearly 5,000 former mill dogs, and even though it is far from a population center, it has attracted more than 800 volunteers. It now has partnerships with groups in six states that care for and place former mill dogs, but I do not know if there is one here in Michigan. There ought to be a law against these mill dog breeders who care so little about their animals. Frankly, I would like our firm to start a lawsuit against any of those mill breeder dogs in Michigan.

A CANINE FRIEND DOES A BODY GOOD!

Bob was nice enough to bring me back an article from the *Salt Lake City Tribune* of July 31, 2011, entitled "A canine friend does a body good." The article's sub-headline is that "Having a dog can help lower your blood pressure and cholesterol and encourage the active lifestyle necessary to staying healthy." At the same time, having a human helps us dogs keep sharp and assist in our exercise and nutrition. As the article says, having a dog around does more than just make you smile. Of course, having a human around makes us want to lick and kiss even more as I personally prefer humans over dogs. If you are interested in reading the article, contact my website and we will try to get you one.

PETS ARE GOOD FOR THE HANDICAPPED

I just heard about a case in Connecticut where a condominium had a regulation prohibiting pets in all units. A lady moved in and asked that her dog be allowed because an animal was prescribed to her because she suffers from a mental illness. The board rejected the explanation, and she filed suit against the association. Apparently, the board was not aware of the Federal Fair Housing Act, which prohibits discrimination housing against, among other classes, handicapped persons, and she is handicapped if she has a physical or mental impairment. I have been waiting to see how the case turns out, but most associations should be aware of the fact that we dogs can be of great help to people who have physical and mental disabilities.

JOYLEIH'S COMMENTS

NEED MORE DOG PARKS

Once in a while I get to peruse *USA Today* and noted that an article entitled "Dogs get run of more city parks" suggests that dog parks, where we can roam freely without a tether, are the fastest-growing segment of city parks. Portland, Oregon, had the highest per capita number of off-leash dog parks among the nation's 100 largest cities. I personally like dog parks because it is a good place for socializing—like the Bonita Beach dog park. The article also mentions a series of guidebooks for dog owners. I like what the author said that dog owners have become a powerful lobby and "owners feel that 'these children of ours are furry, they have four legs, but we are still paying taxes to be here and we still want our recreational needs met.' " I also like the fact that the article referred to "pooch power" in getting dog parks, and I hope that Detroit and its suburbs will become more dog friendly.

THE POTBELLIED PIG "WILBUR"

Bailley has asked me to do a commentary regarding a potbellied pig at a condominium. I am advised that there are an estimated one million unwanted feral hogs running amok in Texas. Obviously, the governor of Texas hasn't taken control of that issue. One pig named Wilbur is not one of them. Wilbur is a Vietnamese potbellied pig whose owners happen to live in a homeowner association. Wilbur is not the main course for dinner, but rather a pet-like companion. The association's rules do not consider Wilbur a pet. The board gave Wilbur's custodians a month to find another home, threatening a $200 a day fine if they did not comply, but Wilbur's custodians have hired a lawyer who argues that he is not livestock because he is not used for food or other labor and because potbellied pig jowl is taxed in Texas because it is livestock feed. Now I happen to think that Wilbur, his custodians and his lawyer have a good argument. I think Wilbur ought to stay. Apparently, Wilbur has his own website and Facebook page which I will be happy to give you if you e-mail me. I am sick and tired of Bailley getting all of the e-mails, so hopefully I will receive a few.

THE POWER OF PETS

Now, I know from what Bob barks at me, I do a lot of running around the house and get into a lot of trouble, but I am also aware of the fact that there is a national fitness program by Mars Pet Care entitled "The Power of Pets." It aims to get families and pets walking and playing together. It debuted at various YMCAs in Brooklyn, New York; Chicago; Washington, D.C.; Nashville; and Portland, Ore. Unfortunately, there is not one in Michigan. Mars Pet Care, through its Waltham Center for Pet Nutrition, sponsors research on the benefits of human-animal interaction. Recent studies show that children who have pets are more active, and seniors who walk dogs are healthier than seniors who rely on human partners for exercise. It is my view that having a pet does help people become more active, and having a human helps us become more active; otherwise I would probably be sitting around all day in a cage and not handling my assistant legal beagle duties as efficiently as I do.

DOGS ARE GOOD FOR YOUR HEALTH

As many of you may know, *USA Today* often has complimentary articles about dogs in its paper. I was read a recent article that appeared on Thursday, Oct. 14, 2010, about my fellow dogs being trained to detect low blood sugar levels in children. It just goes to show you how valuable we are in improving the health of our human friends while providing them with, of course, unconditional love and licks. I am also advised that beagles have been at the forefront in helping to determine the accuracy of drugs for humans, but I am glad that that practice has seemed to stop. It is getting a little more chilly here in Michigan, so I will probably have more time to stay in and do my legal chores, especially when the snow comes, so you may be seeing more commentaries coming from me, though probably not as much as from Bailley, who works on these things daily.

TAKE YOUR DOG TO DINNER!

Gosh, I am not that old, but I am really excited about reading the article in *USA Today* for Thursday, July 22, 2010, on page 4D: "Take Your Dog to Dinner." Art Smith, of the Art and Soul restaurant in Washington, D.C., says "to appreciate food and life is to appreciate animals, too." Obviously, more restaurants are opening their doors to us, and it is about time. I am tired of having to wait in the car or stay home and get stuck with dog bones when I could be eating at a first-class restaurant, particularly in Florida or California, where they welcome us with more frequency and gratitude than some other places such as here in Michigan. On the other hand, I just learned that a mall in Bloomfield Township has seats outdoors in the hallway and now invites dogs to come for lunch and dinner. That is a great improvement, and I also recognize a recent article in *Travel & Leisure* that speaks about dog hotels, spas, and canine cooking. Again, it is about time, and congratulations to *USA Today* for being progressive and dog worldly.

GREYHOUNDS PROVIDE COMFORT TO VICTIMS OF TRAGEDIES

One of my favorite things to do when I get up on a Wednesday morning is to read, generally, Section D of *USA Today* that has a page devoted to dogs and other pets. I noticed in the June 30, 2010, edition that my brethren, the greyhounds, are being used by an organization to help persons who have been subjected to tragedies in order to take their mind off the tragedy for a period of time by bringing the greyhounds to visit the victims and their helpers. I don't have any personal friends that are greyhounds who do this, but I know that they are great dogs for this kind of activity, and I know that dogs in general can divert the attention of humans from the everyday rigors and stresses of working and living by giving us a pat on the back, taking us for a walk, playing with us, giving us big hugs and kisses, and by us providing a good lick or two in return. Congratulations to those humans who allow us to bring rest and comfort to those who have been subjected to tragedy such as Hurricane Katrina and similar disasters.

P.S. If I could lick up the oil in the Gulf of Mexico, I would.

EPILOGUE

My critics may again say that I have been too quick to criticize condo operations and that this further analysis is not as a constructive as it might have been. Perhaps I may again be thought of as arrogant and/or condescending. There may be some truth in that. I would argue, however, that if one reads this new edition and observes the dynamics of condo operation as they really are, they would see that there is still much room for improvement. And let me say, at the risk of sounding like a politician, that I have advanced and achieved a solid program for prosperity and the betterment of the condominium association which, when implemented, has been successful for our firm's clients over the years.

The initial edition of this book has been received well, and I hope that this new edition will further serve as a standard text for persons who want to know what it's really like to live in a condo. I hope they will read this book *before* they buy a condo. I hope directors read this book before they agree to serve on boards or if elected as a director or officer, will refer to this book as a constant source of reference and inspiration. I hope developers read this book before they undertake to develop a condo. I hope management consultants, insurance consultants, accountants and lawyers read this book before they assume the responsibilities and tasks of counseling and/or representing condo associations, co-owners, and/or developers.

What motivated me to write the initial book and then this updated text was, in part, a need to share my personal trials and tribulations of more than 40 years with condominium and community associations. Admittedly, writing these books was therapeutic, and to that extent it has served its purpose. If the book again serves to open the eyes of condo purchasers, condo developers, condo board members, officers, management companies, and service-related people, it will again have far exceeded my fondest hopes and expectations.

ACKNOWLEDGMENTS

As with my first book, which allowed me to meet many new people at book signings and other speaking engagements for which I am greatly appreciative, I must give recognition to a number of individuals who participated in helping me draft the revised edition of *CONDO LIVING 2: The Authoritative Guide to Buying, Selling, and Operating a Condominium*. In addition to those people who are recognized in my initial book, I wanted to give particular recognition to persons in my firm who helped me update and add various chapters and appendixes to this book which I believe will be extraordinarily helpful to the reader, whatever their affiliation may be with a condominium development. Brian Harris, an associate of mine with the law firm was very helpful in putting together a number of the chapters that have been added to the book. Obviously, M. Katherine Michael continues to be an invaluable aid, having been with our firm heading into her third decade. Also, as I acknowledged in my initial book, I want to give thanks to those who have crossed my path, both good and bad, over the 40 years in which I have been in the condominium field. Whether or not we were on the same page or on the same wave length, they inspired me to add my additional thoughts in this new book to help those who are interested in condominium living and/or who are now or will be involved in the governance of condominium and other community associations. To all of you, I give my sincerest thanks and gratitude.

Lastly, but not at all intended to be least, thanks to Bailley and Joyleih who have become an integral part of my life as legal beagles and as companions. They have contributed greatly to my peace of mind as well as the quality of life which I enjoy. However, our legal beagles would not be able to assist me without the encouragement and love which I received from Anita Mitton, who has allowed me the sense of freedom to express my thoughts without reservation and has encouraged me in my law practice and personal life to enjoy life to the fullest. Bailley and Joyleih would not be part of my life if it were not for Anita who, like my children, one a doctor and the other a lawyer, have been there to listen to my condo stories, some good and some bad for these many years.

ABOUT THE AUTHOR

Robert Meisner is a practicing attorney and licensed real estate broker who received a B.A. from the University of Michigan and a J.D. from the University of Michigan Law School and is a member of the Honor Society of Phi Kappa Phi. Meisner has been an attorney licensed to practice in Michigan since 1969 and has been honored as a Super Lawyer in the State of Michigan for a number of years. He has been an adjunct professor in condominium and community association law at Cooley Law School and Michigan State University Law School and has taught condominium and community association courses offered to directors, officers, managers, and developers of community associations through various universities and colleges in Michigan.

Meisner has also lectured widely through the Community

Association Institute on a national level, as well as at the Community Association Institute Local Chapter in Michigan, the Institute of Continuing Legal Education sponsored by the State Bar of Michigan and United Condominium Owners of Michigan, where he has been general counsel since its inception in 1973. He is a widely published columnist with the Hometown Newspapers-Observer and Eccentric Newspapers authoring a column on real estate for more than 35 years. Meisner was also a co-draftsperson of the 1978 Condominium Act of Michigan, the Amendments to the Condominium Act in Michigan in 2001 and 2002, and has concentrated his law practice in the area of community association and condo law as well as commercial litigation. Meisner is a senior member of The Meisner Law Group, P.C. Meisner practices law in Bingham Farms, Michigan, and represents community and condominium associations, developers, and co-owners throughout the State of Michigan.

INDEX

A

abandoned, 183–185

advisory committee, 124, 129, 138, 139

affiliations, 57, 117. *See also* conflicts of interest

air space, 17–18, 157, 197

American Pet Products Manufacturers Association, 238

animals, 39, 163, 238, 240, 243

annoyance, 165–166, 168, 188, 190

apathy, propensity for, 110, 210, 218, 231

arsenic, 156

articles of incorporation, 20, 50

asbestos, 156

assessment, 4, 22–24, 37, 43–44, 48, 52, 54, 56, 60, 75, 78– 79,
    81–82, 95, 97, 101, 106, 111, 122–123, 130–132, 140–141,
    143, 152–153, 155, 171–173, 175–176, 178, 183, 198, 200,
    216–218, 222–223, 229, 234, 236
assessment collection, 172
association bylaws, 20, 50
associations, *see also* board of directors
    defined, 15–19, 25
    documents, 19–20
    management of, 21–22
    need for, 137–138
attached condominium, 7–8, 38, 165
audits, 129–134, 139, 149, 152, 230

B
board of directors,
    role of, 105–106
    subcommitees, 109
boat, 18, 35, 51, 65–66, 69, 158
budget, association, 55
buying considerations,
    board of directors, 106
    lifestyle, 3, 39
    ownership, definition of, 17, 48
bylaws, 19–20

C
California, 29–30
campsite condominium, 17, 62, 63
capital gains, 85–87
children, 3, 7–8, 38, 92–96, 165, 191–193, 241, 243
Civil Relief Act, 31
closing, 54, 77, 81–84, 195

commercial condominium, 17, 60–61, 64, 197
committee structure, 109–111
common elements, 6–7, 18–24, 43–45, 48, 78–79, 82, 95,
    106–108, 112, 122–123, 132–133, 153, 165, 178, 188,
    190–191, 198, 215, 232–235
Common Ground Magazine, 238
communal living, 35–36, 162
community association, 25, 31–33, 36, 105, 109–110, 112–113,
    116, 143–145, 147, 209, 211, 224, 227, 236–237
community association attorney, 33
Community Associations Institute, 32, 145
Condominium Act, 16, 49, 54, 182, 230, 232
Condominium Buyers Handbook, 50, 51
condominium bylaws, 19, 20, 50
condominium documents, 18–19, 21, 23 – 24, 28, 30, 47–48,
    50–51, 54, 56, 62–63, 65, 76–82, 84–85, 91–92, 94–95, 97,
    106–108, 115–116, 118, 122–124, 128, 131–132, 139–140,
    143, 158, 162, 165–169, 187, 191, 198–200, 208–209, 216,
    218, 231, 233
conflict of interest, 123, 139, 142, 228
conversion condominium, 43– 45, 53, 131
cooling-off period, 51
cooperative, 16, 25, 84, 86, 147
co-ops, 38, 116
co-owners, defined, 18
corporate bylaws, 20
CPA, 131, 141, 152

D

date of possession, 83
declaration, 18–19, 35, 51, 65–66, 69, 158, 225
defunct developer, 183
delinquency cap, 198

deregulation, 28-30, 208
disabled persons, 132
disclaimer of warranties, 44
disclosure statement, 43, 45, 53–57
discrimination, 8, 31, 157, 234, 241

E
environment, 35–36, 38, 156, 158, 240
equity, 4, 41, 46–47, 62, 169, 231
eviction, 95, 99, 101

F
Fair Housing Act, 7, 157, 200, 241
Federal Emergency Management Agency, 198
Federal Fair Housing Act, 7, 157, 241
Federal Fair Housing Amendments, 31
Federal Housing Administration (FHA), 78, 80, 108, 195 – 196, 197, 198, 199, 200, 201, 202, 232, 233
Federal Housing & Economic Recovery Act, 195
Federal Telecommunications Act, 31
FHA Cap, 197
FHA certification, 196–202, 232
FHLMC, 78
fiduciary responsibility, 119, 172, 202
fireworks, 191
flood insurance, 198
FNMA, 78
foreclosure, 23, 96, 100, 169, 172–174, 176, 178, 200
fraud, 150

G
gardening, 167
garnishment, 177, 231

Golden Rule, 219
governance, 36, 114, 116, 151–152, 208

H
hazard insurance, 198
high-rise condominium, 41, 191
home warranty, 229
hotel condominium, 64 – 65
Housing and Urban Development, 197

I
indemnification, 148, 153
industrial condominium, 17
Institute of Real Property Management, The, 145
insurance, 52, 60, 84, 107, 109, 117, 123, 132, 148–149, 150,
    152–153, 157, 165, 185, 188, 198–200, 215, 220, 223, 229,
    235, 248
Internal Revenue Code, 69, 85, 87–88
Internal Revenue Service, 85 – 86
investment property, 59
investor ownership limit, 198
IRS Publication 523, 85

L
lease agreement, 91–92, 97–100, 163
liability insurance, 123, 132, 198
lien, 23, 84, 96, 143, 148, 169, 173–174, 213
limited liability company, 60, 183
listing agreement, 77–78
loss limitation, 72
low-income housing, 37

M

maintenance fee, 56
management company, 22, 25, 57, 77, 107–108, 111, 127, 129, 130, 134, 140, 144–152, 178, 190, 208, 210, 220, 223, 225, 228
management contract, 147–148
managing agent, 8, 19, 22, 57, 93, 96, 144, 150, 152, 157, 166, 190, 192, 213, 228
marina condominium, 65–66
master deed, 18–21, 35, 50–51, 65–66, 69, 158, 198–199
Michigan Condominium Act, 16, 54, 182, 230, 232
Michigan Department of Labor and Economic Growth, 50
mixed-use condominium, 63
mobile home, 18, 61–63, 69, 86
mobile home condominium, 17, 61
modification agreement, 82
mold, 96, 109, 156, 231
motorcycles, 166–167
multi-dwelling condominiums, 197
Murphy's Law, 218

N

new construction, 42–47, 49
noise, 5, 7, 168, 188–190, 192
nuisance, 165–166, 168, 188, 190

O

Observer & Eccentric, 10, 227
operational procedures, 122–123
outside professionals, 137
owner occupancy requirement, 197

P

parking lot condominium, 17, 65

Parkinson's Law, 218

personalities, 7, 109, 113, 146, 162

personal use, 63, 70–72

Peter Principle, 217

pets, 24, 163, 241–244

pit bulls, 164, 238–239

Planned Unit Development (PUD), 24–25

purchase agreement, 43, 46–47, 49–54, 56–57, 78–79, 81–85, 230

R

radon gas, 155–156

religious beliefs, 234

religious discrimination, 234

rental restrictions, 97

resale condominium, 46–47, 53

reservation agreement, 49–50

reserve fund, 4, 198–199, 232

reserves, 42, 45, 49, 122, 131, 133, 213, 222, 232

resident manager, 130, 148

right of first refusal, 54, 79–80, 200

S

second home, 59–60, 207

Section 1031, 87–88

short sale, 236

site condominium, 5, 7, 9, 17–18, 21, 197, 232–233

soil contaminants, 156

statute, 16, 19, 24, 28–31, 46, 52, 100–101, 132, 216, 225

steering committee, 124–129

subdivision plan, 20, 50

T
tax deductions, 70, 73
termination, 147–148
terrorist, 111
time-share condominium, 17, 64–65, 197
title insurance, 84
townhouse condominium, 41

U
Uniform Condominium Act, 16
United Condominium Owners of Michigan, 32
United States Code, 200
United States Department of Justice, 238
uri-formaldehyde, 156

V
VA, 80

W
water rights, 66, 157

Z
zoning, 24

REFERENCES

1. The Meisner Law Group, P.C.: www.meisner-law.com;

2. American Bar Association, public resources page:
www.abanet.org/public.html

3. Community Associations Institute: www.caionline.org

4. United Condominium Owners of Michigan:
www.ucomonline.org

5. Twelve-Pack: A series of form procedures, rules and agreements
custom drafted by The Meisner Law Group, P.C. law firm designed
to supplement the condominium documents of a particular project

and to facilitate its operations, and which includes a Delinquent Assessment Collection Policy, a Bylaw (and Rules) Enforcement Policy, a Fine Procedure, Rules and Regulations Regarding Satellite Dishes and Antennas, two (2) Agreements to Modify Common Elements for Standard Modifications and for Persons With Disabilities, a form Lease Agreement, a form Service Contract, an Employee Manual, a Code of Conduct for Boards of Directors, a Maintenance Matrix, a Current Condominium Document Booklet and CD of Documents, and an Electronic Notification Authorization Form.

6. "Condominium Operation: Getting Started and Staying on the Right Track," 2nd Edition (2002) by Robert M. Meisner

For copies of the above booklet or to contact the author:

Robert M. Meisner Founding Member
The Meisner Law Group, P.C.
30200 Telegraph Road Suite 467
Bingham Farms, MI 48025-4506

e-mail: bmeisner@meisner-law.com
Web: www.meisner-law.com
(248) 644-4433

7. Bailley and Joyleih, web page, www.meisner-law.com

8. *Observer & Eccentric* Articles.
www.hometownlife.com/section/REALESTATE

9. Article "Divided Loyalties" *Common Ground* Magazine, September/October 2009, by Robert M. Meisner.